PENGUIN BOOKS

# THE DESERT YEAR

Joseph Wood Krutch was the author of numerous books, perhaps the three best known being *The Modern Temper, Samuel Johnson,* and *Henry David Thoreau.*

# The Desert Year

# The Desert Year

JOSEPH WOOD KRUTCH

*Decorations by*
*Rudolf Freund*

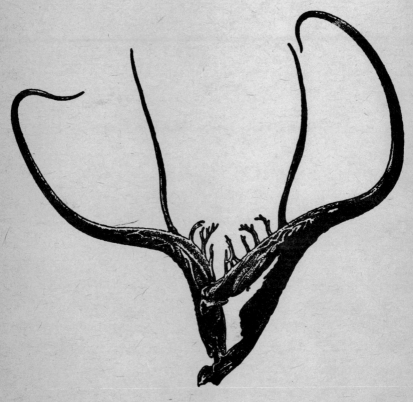

PENGUIN BOOKS

Penguin Books Ltd, Harmondsworth,
Middlesex, England
Penguin Books, 625 Madison Avenue,
New York, New York 10022, U.S.A.
Penguin Books Australia Ltd, Ringwood,
Victoria, Australia
Penguin Books Canada Ltd, 41 Steelcase Road West,
Markham, Ontario, Canada
Penguin Books (N.Z.) Ltd, 182–190 Wairau Road,
Auckland 10, New Zealand

First published in the United States of America by
William Sloane Associates, Inc., 1952
Viking Compass Edition published 1963
Reprinted 1964, 1966, 1968, 1969, 1970, 1971, 1972, 1973, 1975
Published in Penguin Books 1977

ISBN 0 14 00.4448 5

Printed in the United States of America by
Offset Paperback Mfrs., Inc., Dallas, Pennsylvania
Set in Linotype Caledonia

For Helen d'Autremont, without whom this book might never have been written.

The author wishes to thank *Commentary, House and Garden,* and *Virginia Quarterly Review* for permission to reprint portions of this volume which originally appeared in those magazines.

# Contents

# The Desert Year

# Chapter One

# Why I Came

# Why I Came

Scenery, as such, never meant much to me. A city man to begin with, I never thought "beauty spots" worth the trouble it took to go look at them. This mountain rises ten thousand feet; that waterfall drops fifteen hundred. What, I replied inwardly, is to prevent it? A week later I had nothing in my mind which could not have got there via a picture postcard. A pot on the window sill or a goldfish on the desk meant more.

Then, having lived somewhat unwillingly in a quiet countryside for a year and a half, I made the great and obvious discovery which thousands must have made before me. There is all the difference in the world between looking at something and living

3

with it. In nature, one never really sees a thing for the first time until one has seen it for the fiftieth. It never means much until it has become part of some general configuration, until it has become not a "view" or a "sight" but an integrated world of which one is a part; until one is what the biologist would call part of a biota.

A "tour" is like a cocktail party. One "meets" everybody and knows no one. I doubt that what is ordinarily called "travel" really does broaden the mind any more than a cocktail party cultivates the soul. Perhaps the old-fashioned tourist who used to check off items in his Baedeker lest he forget that he had seen them was not legitimately so much a figure of fun as he was commonly made. At best, more sophisticated travelers usually know only the fact that they have seen something, not anything worth keeping which they got from the sight itself. Chartres is where the lunch was good; Lake Leman where we couldn't get a porter. To have lived in three places, perhaps really to have lived in only one, is better than to have seen a hundred. I am a part, said Ulysses, of all that I have known—not of all that I have visited or "viewed."

In defense of cocktail parties it is commonly said that they are not ends in themselves but only, more or less frankly, occasions on which people offer themselves for inspection by their fellows. Young men and young women attend in order, as they say, "to look 'em over"; older people in order, as they more sedately put it, on the chance of meeting someone whose acquaintance they would like to cultivate. Something of the same sort is the most that can be said in defense of the tour. Of some spot of earth one may feel that one would like it if one could really see or really know it.

Here, one may say, I should like to stay for a month, or a year, or a decade. It could give something to me and I, perhaps, something to it—if only some sort of love and understanding. More rarely—perhaps only once, perhaps two or three times—one experiences something more like love at first sight. The desire to stay, to enter in, is not a whim or a notion but a passion. *Verweile doch, du bist so schön!* If I do not somehow possess this, if I never learn what it was that called out, what it was that was being offered, I shall feel all my life that I have missed something intended for me. If I do not, for a time at least, live here I shall not have lived as fully as I had the capacity to live.

A dozen years ago I had such an experience on a trip undertaken without much enthusiasm. I had got off the train at Lamy, New Mexico and started in an automobile across the rolling semidesert toward Albuquerque. Suddenly a new, undreamed of world was revealed. There was something so unexpected in the combination of brilliant sun and high, thin, dry air with a seemingly limitless expanse of sky and earth that my first reaction was delighted amusement. How far the ribbon of road beckoned ahead! How endlessly much there seemed to be of the majestically rolling expanse of bare earth dotted with sagebrush! How monotonously repetitious in the small details, how varied in shifting panorama! Unlike either the Walrus or the Carpenter, I laughed to see such quantities of sand.

Great passions, they say, are not always immediately recognized as such by their predestined victims. The great love which turns out to be only a passing fancy is no doubt commoner than the passing fancy which turns out to be a great love, but one phenomenon is not for that reason any less significant than the other. And when I try to remember my first delighted response to the charms of this great, proud, dry, and open land I think not so much of Juliet recognizing her fate the first time she laid eyes upon him but of a young cat I once introduced to the joys of catnip.

He took only the preoccupied, casual, dutiful sniff which was the routine response to any new object presented to his attention before he started to walk away. Then he did what is called in the slang of the theater "a double take." He stopped dead in his tracks; he turned incredulously back and inhaled a

6

good noseful. Incredulity was swallowed up in delight. Can such things be? Indubitably they can. He flung himself down and he wallowed.

For three successive years following my first experience I returned with the companion of my Connecticut winters to the same general region, pulled irresistibly across the twenty-five hundred miles between my own home and this world which would have been alien had it not almost seemed that I had known and loved it in some previous existence. From all directions we crisscrossed New Mexico, Arizona, and southern Utah, pushing as far south as the Mexican border, as far west as the Mojave Desert in California. Guides led us into the unfrequented parts of Monument Valley and to unexplored cliff dwellings in a mesa canyon the very existence of which was nowhere officially recorded at the time. We climbed the ten thousand foot peak of Navajo Mountain to look from its summit across the vast unexplored land of rocks which supported, they said, not one inhabitant, white or Indian. Then one day we were lost from early morning to sunset when the tracks we were following in the sand petered out to leave us alone in the desert between Kayenta and the Canyon de Chelly.

To such jaunts the war put an end. For seven years I saw no more of sand and sunshine and towering butte. Meanwhile I lived as happily as one could

expect to live in such years. The beautiful world of
New England became again my only world. I was
not sure that I should ever return to the new one I
had discovered. Indeed it receded until I was uncertain whether I had ever seen it at all except in that
previous existence some memory of which seemed to
linger when, for the first time in this one, I met it
face to face. Now and then, on some snowy night
when the moon gleamed coldly on the snow, I woke
from a dream of sun and sand, and when I looked
from my window moon and snow were like the pale
ghosts of sand and sun.

At last, for the fifth time, I came again, verifying
the fact that remembered things did really exist.
But I was still only a traveler or even only the traveler's vulgar brother, the tourist. No matter how often I
looked at something I did no more than look. It was
only a view or a sight. It threatened to become familiar without being really known and I realized
that what I wanted was not to look at but to live with
this thing whose fascination I did not understand.
And so, a dozen years after I first looked I have come
for the sixth time; but on this occasion to live for
fifteen months in a world which will, I hope, lose the
charm of the strange only to take on the more powerful charm of the familiar.

Certainly I do not know yet what it is that this
land, together with the plants and animals who find

its strangenesses normal, has been trying to say to me for twelve years, what kinship with me it is that they all so insistently claim. I know that many besides myself have felt its charm, but I know also that not all who visit it do, that there are, indeed, some in whom it inspires at first sight not love but fear, or even hatred. Its appeal is not the appeal of things universally attractive, like smiling fields, bubbling springs, and murmuring brooks. To some it seems merely stricken, and even those of us who love it recognize that its beauty is no easy one. It suggests patience and struggle and endurance. It is courageous and happy, not easy or luxurious. In the brightest colors of its sandstone canyons, even in the brightest colors of its brief spring flowers, there is something austere.

Within the general area which called to me there is the greatest variety possible, once one grants the constant factors: much sun and little rain. The most spectacular part is the high region to the north, where the plateau is at about five thousand feet and mountains, here and there, rise to reach twelve thousand. Across the southernmost and most frequented part of this northern plateau the Grand Canyon cuts its way, and to the northeast of the canyon, in the region given over mostly to the Indian reservations, rock sculpture becomes most fantastic. It is here that the windblown sand has carved the rock—red and yellow and white —into the isolated "monuments" which stand out in the clear air to produce "objects in space" which the nonobjective sculptor can hardly hope to imitate, at least on so grand a scale.

To the south, when one drops off the plateau—and for many miles there is no descent other than that of an almost literal drop—one lands in an extension of Mexico's Sonoran Desert. Curious little heaps of mountain—the remains, I suppose, of what were once ranges—are scattered here and there over the otherwise flat land. This is the country of cactus and mesquite and creosote bush. Hotter in summer, warmer in winter, than the higher parts, it is the region most properly called desert country. It is also less varied than the other, less tumultuously exciting, and more fit for the kind of human habitation we know. It is capable, as the northern part is not, of being taken possession of by human beings and used to support a moderate population.

Yet something—perhaps something more than the grand common factors of much sun and little rain —links the two regions, makes them part of the same world, enables them to exercise some kindred charm. But what, I ask myself again, is the true nature, the real secret of that charm? I am no simple stoic. Hardship and austerity do not in themselves make an inevitable appeal to me and they are not only, not even principally, what I seek here. Everywhere there is also some kind of gladness.

Perhaps some of this glad charm is physical. To many people at least, dry warmth gives a sense of well-being and is in its own way as stimulating to them as the frosty air of the north is to others, caressing rather than whipping them into joyous activity. Some more of the charm is, I am sure, aesthetic. The way in which both desert and plateau use form and color is as different from the way in which more conventionally picturesque regions use them, as the way of the modern painter is different from that of the academician. But there is also, I am sure, a spiritual element. Nature's way here, her process and her moods, correspond to some mood which I find in myself. Or, if that sounds too mystical for some tastes, we can, perhaps, compromise on a different formulation. Something in myself can be projected upon the visible forms which nature assumes here. She permits me to suppose that she is expressing something which another much-loved countryside left, for all the richness of the things it did express, unsaid, even unsuggested. To try to find out what that may be is the reason I have come once more to look at, to listen to, and, this time if possible, to be more intimately a part of, something whose meaning I have sensed but not understood.

Now that I am here I still know no better than I

knew before what that something is. All I do know is that the reality or the power to produce an illusion is still present. I know also that the first hints of its existence began, as usual, to be unmistakably whispered in that transition zone between the world I was leaving and the world I was coming to.

This time, as always before except on the very first visit, we drove all the way by automobile, watching eagerly in order not to miss the first phenomenon which would announce the beginning of fundamental novelty. But how, when the important thing is a configuration, can one decide when the elements added one to one have established it? Certainly neither Arkansas nor Missouri is part of the Southwest, though the sky seems to expand, once one has crossed the Mississippi at Memphis or at Cairo. State boundaries will not serve to define because they do not quite correspond to geographical realities. In one latitude, southeastern New Mexico is only a somewhat drier Texas; a little farther north, the westernmost parts of Texas are really New Mexico. And yet along either approach there comes a moment when one hesitates no longer and must say with full conviction "We have arrived."

Mr. Bernard DeVoto, downright and specific as usual, maintains that there is a sensible answer to the sentimental question with which poets and luncheon clubs have delighted to fumble, "Where does the West begin?" "The West begins where the average annual rainfall drops below twenty inches. When you reach the line which marks that drop—for convenience, the one-hundredth meridian—you have reached the West." My own less compact definition concerns itself with the individual phenomena, for some of which this drop in rainfall is responsible. But Mr. DeVoto's straight line, which runs near the western border of Oklahoma, at least cuts here and there across the zigzag which I should draw. And it is also worth noting that a leading ornithologist, Roger Tory Peterson, reaches independently the same conclusion as Mr. DeVoto. At the one-hundredth meridian western species of birds begin to predominate over the eastern.

On one route which I have several times taken, the change in the look of the land takes place suddenly and dramatically. West of Amarillo, but still in Texas and only two or three degrees west of Mr. DeVoto's line, the road dips suddenly to drop from one plateau to another only a hundred or a hundred and fifty feet lower. This drop is barely enough to register on a pocket altimeter, yet it separates two strongly contrasted landscapes. On top there is the plain of Texas, dryish but undramatic. Below, the red, eroded sandstone and the cactus, which one has not seen before declare that this is New Mexico a good many miles before the map makers have recognized the fact.

On the slightly more southern route which I took this time, one must wait a little longer, though that is mostly because one has been moving southwest rather than due west. At almost exactly the same meridian line there is the crest of a hill crowned by a gas station which the poetic proprietor has named High Lonesome; and from that point one looks down on the first real desert. Shortly after we had passed the crest the first lizard scuttled across the roadway and a few minutes later a road-runner, the most comic of desert fowl, raced our car for a few moments.

Half a mile farther down, another bird of the same species strode contentedly along with nine inches of snake hanging out of his mouth, to remind me of a grotesque if not particularly poetic fact about these gawky birds who have renounced most of the traditions of the cuckoo family to which they are said to belong. One frequently sees them with a snake thus dangling, because a snake is usually too long to be swallowed all at once. Accordingly, after doing their best, they go about all day nonchalantly swallowing an inch or two more of reptile from time to time as the lower end digests away. Not infrequently the snake is a rattler, but harmless varieties and even lizards will do as well.

These road-runners are cocky fellows who have

managed to make a virtue out of their clownish gait and manners. Nothing else that lives in the desert, not even a spiny cactus or a resinous creosote bush, seems more at home there. I am reminded that I must take him in too, that majesty and sublimity are not the whole story, that wherever there is life there is also unconscious absurdity and, at least on man's level, conscious comedy. It is well, I think, that the road-runner should greet me at the beginning. This is his country and there is probably no one who could better teach me about it.

# *Chapter Two*

# What It Looks Like

# What It Looks Like

During those years when I was a mere tourist in the Southwest most of my sightseeing was done in the more spectacular northern part. If one has time only to look, there is more to be looked at there. Probably, before my year is up, I shall return to that incredible land of monoliths through which one moves in perpetual astonishment. It was there that a new kind of grandeur first shocked me into recognition and there, perhaps, that what I can only call the Southwestern Style—old as Egypt and new as modern sculpture—reaches its climax.

Superficially, the more livable southern desert is also less astonishing and more monotonous. Though bare, jagged mountains ultimately close nearly every vista, the desert itself lies peaceful in the sun and repeats with tireless satisfaction its two themes—either cactus, paloverde, mesquite, and sand, or yucca, agave, and ocotillo, the one on the flats, the other on the slopes. It has discovered its modes and it sticks to them; content to do what it can do, indifferent to your attention or lack of it. Love me or hate me, the desert seems to say, this is what I am and this is what I shall remain. Go north for astonishment if you must have it. What I offer is different.

What one finds, after one has come to take for granted the grand general simplicity, will be what one takes the trouble to look for—the brilliant little flower springing improbably out of the bare, packed sand, the lizard scuttling with incredible speed from cactus clump to spiny bush, the sudden flash of a bright-colored bird. This dry world, all of which seems so strange to you, is normal to them. It is their paradise, their universe as-it-ought-to-be. Can you, like them, not merely look, but live spiritually here? Can this seemingly difficult land, which nevertheless flourishes vigorously and lives joyously, come to seem to you not merely strange and interesting but as normal as the icy winter and almost too riotous summers you have taken for granted? Those questions are part of what I want to answer for myself and are in part why I have settled down for a while in the very middle of a stretch of Lower Sonoran Desert.

By fortunate accident I have found the ideal spot
—a house not ten miles from a medium-sized town
but plump in the middle of hundreds of acres of desert, untouched except for an occasional artificial
oasis where someone has put a home. To the north,
only a mile or two away, rises a bold range of mountains, bare except for the scattered green dots which
represent some clump of unconquerable shrubbery.
In every other direction, the vista is closed only at
the horizon's edge, to which the nearly level desert
stretches away.

The tall, branching, and twisted columns of the
giant saguaro cactus are all about me and through
binoculars I can see them striding half-way up the
nearest mountain side. They are the most obviously
strange, the most plainly theatrical feature of the
landscape. Understandably, they have been popu-
larized as curiosities, yet despite this popularization
they will probably be the last familiar sight to be
really accepted as familiar, to be believed in and
taken for granted as natural and normal rather than
as part of some stage setting. Before I arrived their
white blossoms had faded. At this moment, their
prickly-pearlike fruits, stuck improbably at the ends of
the improbable columns, are showing bright red
against the sky as the ripe ends burst open and the
birds eagerly pluck out the seeds.

If I step through the gate in my patio wall, I am in

a moment in a kind of sparse wilderness which shows no sign of man's intrusion, which belongs still to the creatures who have always lived here. Besides the animals there are many green, growing things of many kinds. There are cacti, of course, and among them the great barrels which would be specimens in any botanical garden and which, at first, surprise me as much as, in Africa, I should no doubt be surprised to see lions and elephants not attached to any zoo or circus. There are also the flat green pads of the more familiar "prickly pear" grown to unfamiliar size; there are the coppery purple pads of the somewhat less common Santa Rita prickly pear and also, omnipresent, one or another variety of the cholla—that fierce touch-me-not of the desert which often assumes the form of a low tree with bark on its trunk and branches of savagely armed cylindrical pads. The spines are not the minute spicules we first think of when we think of cacti but much like darning needles in length, in strength, and in sharpness.

At first sight, the other large growing things—the mesquite, the paloverde and the creosote bush—seem less abnormal. From a distance, this stretch of desert floor looks green enough and almost like the thickets one finds in many cooler, damper lands. But there is much which distinguishes it. For one thing, the green is a grayer green. For another, one realizes as soon as one steps into it that it is not really a thicket at all but a floor on which everything must have—and everything has managed to get—its standing room.

There is no continuous carpet of grass or herbage, no crowding together of exuberantly growing plant life. One does not push one's way through undergrowth; one strolls almost as in a garden. Where water is scarce, roots spread far and shallowly. Hence the area to which a mesquite, for example, has successfully established claim will support little else. For a while it is hard to believe that this untouched country has not been thinned by some human gardener. Because of a spacing which nature has attended to, it has a curious air of being a park rather than a wilderness.

In New England the struggle for existence is visibly the struggle of plant with plant, each battling his neighbor for sunlight and for the spot of ground which, so far as moisture and nourishment are concerned, would support them all. Here, the contest is not so much of plant against plant as of plant against inanimate nature. The limiting factor is not the neighbor but water; and I wonder if that is, perhaps, one of the things which makes this country seem to enjoy a kind of peace one does not find elsewhere. The struggle of living thing against living thing can be distressing in a way that a mere battle with the elements is not. If some great clump of cactus dies this summer it will be because the cactus has grown beyond the capacity of its roots to get water, not because one green fellow creature has bested it in some limb-to-limb struggle. In my more familiar East the crowding of the countryside seems almost to parallel the crowding of the cities. Out here there is, even in nature, no congestion.

From my window I see a family of Gambel's quail strolling about like barnyard fowl—the babies much like baby chicks, the mother with the one coquettish plume curled out from the top of her head and bobbing before her eyes. The other day a road-runner leaped to the patio wall to stroll cockily along its rim for a few minutes before deciding that the enclosure offered little promise of either snakes or lizards. Perhaps these and the other small creatures which the desert supports so comfortably are not really much tamer than members of the wild fauna in Connecticut, but the unfamiliarity makes one more aware of them and I cannot yet take the horned toad who looks at me with beady eyes from under a mesquite bush in the same matter-of-fact way that I take a wood frog in the East.

The birds too, of course, are different, and so far I have learned to recognize only the most obvious— the cactus wren who builds his messy, sparrowlike nest among the murderous spines of the cholla a few yards from the front door; the hooded oriole who wears the obligatory orange-and-black livery of his family; the Arizona cardinal, more brilliant than his southeastern cousin; and the woodpeckers who have excavated two or three holes in every saguaro. As I awake in the morning the first thing I am aware of, the first thing which reminds me that I am not in a familiar bed, is some unfamiliar bird voice. At home I would have murmured sleepily "Robin," or "Phoebe," or "Jay" or "Tanager" and gone back to sleep. Here I am aware of something half-way between interest and annoyance, for there is something like mocking challenge in the sound of an unknown bird. I am not one whose imagination accepts very easily the articulate phrases into which the more fanciful translate bird language. A whippoorwill does say "whip-poor-will" and a quail does say "bob white," but that is about as far as I am prepared to go. Here they all say only "Youdontknow whoiam, youdontknow whoiam."

The first sound which even the unobservant stranger is likely to notice, later in the morning or even in the middle of a hot afternoon, is a mysterious, almost threatening coo-uh-cuck-oo breaking the torrid stillness when everything else is quiet. Obviously, I said to myself when I heard it, an owl of some sort. But it turned out to be, of all unlikely things, a dove. White-winged dove is its popular name; it is extremely prevalent; and it loves to sit on the very tip-top of a saguaro. But why a dove, the most banal symbol of the inoffensive and the sentimental, should choose to imitate possibly the fiercest, and certainly the most irascible, of birds I do not know. The suggestion is sinister. It hints at that most terrible of all imaginable anarchies; at that anarchy which, some say, haunted the mind of Shakespeare in *Lear;* the anarchy, I mean, in which everything would forget what is appropriate to its own nature. Are the meek whom the dove symbolizes about to inherit the earth in an unexpected and horrible way—by turning rapacious and implacable? Will the lamb lie down with the lion—and bite him?

In human society, I sometimes suspect that something like that has already begun to happen. As for the dove, his appearance is reassuring. He looks rather pigeonlike and his habits are irreproachable. For all I know, he wants to coo, and perhaps thinks that is what he is doing. Already the knowledge that he does not mean a threat has affected my unconscious reaction and he no longer sounds especially sinister. Moreover, something similar to that has been going on in a grand general way. Much as the idea of this land excited me, much as I wanted to live here for a time, my thoughts of the desert were always tinged by a certain romantic notion that it was, for all its beauty, a hard and difficult land—not, I mean, that I expected any hardship, but merely that I should

be living where nature and her children found it strenuous and difficult to live.

Already I am beginning to wonder how much of
that is a mere projection from my own mind. That
the desert here is mildly austere is certainly true,
and yet neither the plants nor the animals live under
what is, for them, painfully difficult conditions. The
vegetation flourishes in its own way. For the desert
birds and the desert animals this is not an unfavorable environment. They have had to make their
adaptations to the heat and dryness of their land, just
as the animals of other climates made other adaptations to theirs. For the jack rabbit and the ground
squirrel, as well as for the dove and cactus wren, this
is obviously a paradise and there is no paradox in the
smile which the face of the desert wears. Only to
those who come from somewhere else is there anything abnormal about the conditions which prevail.
Only a kind of provincialism will take it for granted
that forty inches of rain is "normal," eight or nine
inches "abnormal." If the paloverde drops its tiny
leaves in the dry season, all the deciduous trees in
wetter, colder countries drop theirs in the cold season, and we do not pity them for it. Moreover, the
paloverde, ingeniously using the green of its trunk
and branches, continues its vital processes during
the drought—which the oak and the elm cannot do

during the cold. Its estivation is partial, not, like the hibernation of northern trees, complete. The little gray chipmunks who scamper over the ground seem quite as gay as their chestnut-brown cousins of the East. If I call this world grim I am obviously indulging in a pathetic fallacy.

We talk about the "adaptation" of the flora and fauna to desert conditions, but "adaptation" is a cold word. Its connotations are mechanical and it alienates us from a life process which is thereby deprived of all emotional meaning. What the plants and animals have actually been doing is analogous to what we do. No matter how much we may try, we cannot really separate our privileges and our predicaments from theirs. To think of them in merely mechanical terms is to come ultimately to think of ourselves in the same terms—and that is precisely what the so-called educated man has been coming more and more to do. But those of us who would rather not deny and renounce the richness of our own experience by thinking of it merely as some process of mechanical adaptation had better not get in the habit of seeing nothing but mechanism in the life histories of other living things.

Let us not say that this animal or even this plant has "become adapted" to desert conditions. Let us say rather that they all have shown courage and ingenuity in making the best of the world as they found it. And let us remember that if to use such terms in connection with them is a fallacy then it can be only somewhat less a fallacy to use the same terms in connection with ourselves. Of the desert flora and fauna, let us also add that the best they have made is a very good best; so good a one, indeed, that we may be sure a desert plant or animal would not want to be any other kind and would languish in what others would call "a more favorable environment." Though there are more ways to kill a cat than by stuffing him with cream that is, nevertheless, one way.

"Desert" is an unfortunate word all around and most of its usual associations are inaccurate as well as unfavorable. In the first place the word doesn't even mean "dry," but simply uninhabited or deserted —like Robinson Crusoe's island. In that sense, the expanse about me is far from being a desert, for it is teeming with live things very glad indeed to be right there. Even in its secondary meaning, "desert" suggests to most people the rolling sand dunes of the Sahara. Something like that one may find in Death Valley; perhaps in parts of the Mojave; and especially, with an added weirdness, in the hundreds of square miles of New Mexico's White Sands, where the great dunes of glistening gypsum drift like the snowbanks one can hardly believe they are not. Most of my Lower Sonoran Desert, however, is not at all like that. The sandy soil is firm and hard-packed; it supports life, less crowded than in wetter regions but pleasantly flourishing. Nature does not frown here. She smiles invitingly.

But I know no term which would do as a substitute. Mary Austin called this the Land of Little Rain and that is better than "desert." Even her phrase is negative; it stresses what the country does not have rather than what it does. Land of Much Sunshine, might almost do. It has at least the advantage of seizing upon an indubitable fact. Land of Too Much Sunshine some might call it; but it is not, for a while at least, too much for those of us who have seldom had enough.

In any event, sun is a primary fact. The other morning when I walked out under a cloudless sky an hour or so before noon I realized that never before in my life had light ever been so bright, so nearly a physical, a tangible presence. It was not yet very hot, not so hot at least that heat rather than light was the dominant fact. But never, in more northern lands or moister atmospheres, is one so flooded with brilliance.

No heat waves disturbed the perfect stillness of the surface. By the eye alone one might almost have supposed it cool. The silvery, new-grown spines of the chollas gleamed with a curious frostiness as the sun poured down its light, along with a strange, radiant, friendly heat. Presently one realized that of this latter there was rather too much. The ardor, like that of certain friendly people, grew gradually almost overwhelming. One decided to retire into one's own shade. But it was still nice to know that such ardor exists.

Yesterday was the summer solstice—the longest day of the year. Three months before that the days had been equal from pole to pole. Since then they had been lengthening in the Northern Hemisphere, shortening in the Southern, and now the process would begin to reverse itself. Yet, paradoxically enough, this longest day was not as long in this hot southern country as it was in New England to the north. It was warmer here not because the sun was shining any longer or even as long but because it shone more directly down from a point more nearly overhead.

That, as I did not realize at the moment, was the cause of that strange brilliance which I had noted. Never before had I been so far south at just this season of the year and therefore never before had I stood under a sun pouring down rays so nearly vertical. Yet even here they are not ever actually vertical, and they never are anywhere north of the Tropic of Cancer. How much more brilliant still noon must be in those real tropics, between Cancer and Capricorn, where the sun can stand precisely overhead!

As at all high altitudes, the temperature here drops quickly when the sun goes down and the nights, except in the very middle of summer, are usually cool. They are also, in the thinnish, dry air, exceptionally brilliant with stars, and the great band of the milky way is unwontedly distinct. On one of my first nights a slender new moon was declining toward the west as the sun sank; for nearly two weeks thereafter I did what I have never done before—watched the moon every night as it grew from the first silvery sliver to its full, round glory. This is an ideal spot for such an enterprise and I suppose that fact tempted me to it, but I was astonished to realize that I had never undertaken it before and astonished at how beautiful and how strange it seemed when one took the trouble to be really aware of what was happening. Every night my moon was about an hour later reaching a given place in the heavens; every night, very noticeably larger; and every night, revealing, through field glasses, more and more of those pits—once called volcanoes but now usually taken for meteor craters—which mark her mysterious surface. One need spend only ten minutes a night to see the show, but one should not miss a phase. On the first evening, the moon offers little competition to the stars; soon, she is indisputably queen of the night. First the milky way yields, then the stars begin to fail one by one, and at the full she has the great bowl almost to herself.

Wondering that I had never really observed these things before I was led to wonder further just how many of the obvious phenomena of the sky I should ever have noticed for myself if no one had ever called my attention to them; if I had been, for example, one of those shepherds of the East who are said to have been the first to take accurate note of them. To be sure, the shepherds had a sky much like this one, and they practiced a solitary profession with plenty of leisure thrown in. But unless I had had at least equally favorable circumstances I am not sure that I should ever have been more than casually aware that the moon was sometimes present and sometimes absent, sometimes crescent and sometimes round. I am not sure that I or—not to be overmodest—most of the people of my acquaintance, would ever have even counted the days of its cycle; and I am equally unsure that I would ever have noticed that the sun rises farther and farther to the north until, after the summer solstice, it begins to retire southward again. I am appalled to think how sluggish science would have been had it been dependent upon me for its beginnings.

Once the moon had passed its full and no longer rose until after my early bedtime, the stars asserted themselves again and I began to take my bearings, to ask just how different this canopy was from the one which normally rolls over me. The answer is simply: "very little indeed." Far as I seem to myself to have traveled, far away as my home country seems, it is actually only about ten of the ninety degrees from pole to equator, and on the perspective of the sky I have hardly moved. Polaris, which marks almost precisely the north, is ten degrees lower toward the horizon, or so at least the books would tell me. But the difference is hardly noticeable. Perhaps Scorpio, at this season and this hour straggling downward in the southern sky, is a little bit more conspicuous, though that, I suspect, is more because the southern horizon is not so shut off by hills than because the constellation is actually very noticeably higher in the heavens.

If I look about me at the landscape, I seem to have traveled a long way and to be in a strange land. If I look above, I am still at home. Any movement or any change is great or trivial, depending upon the point of reference by which one measures it. Over the earth's surface, I have come far; under the sky, I am, for all practical purposes, where I was before. The stars are like a part of that self which, willy-nilly, I brought with me.

Realizing this, I am half-disappointed, half-reassured. To look upward and not find Cassiopeia in her place might be terrifying, almost like finding oneself in an unknown dimension. Of all strangenesses, strange stars must be the hardest to get used to.

# Chapter Three

# How to See It

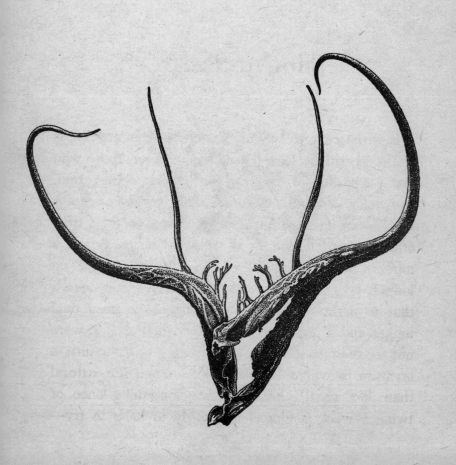

# How to See It

It is not easy to live in that continuous awareness of things which alone is true living. Even those who make a parade of their conviction that sunset, rain, and the growth of a seed are daily miracles are not usually so much impressed by them as they urge others to be. The faculty of wonder tires easily and a miracle which happens everyday is a miracle no longer, no matter how many times one tells oneself that it ought to be. Life would seem a great deal longer and a great deal fuller than it does if it were not for the fact that the human being is, by nature, a creature to whom "*O altitudo*" is much less natural than "So what!". Really to see something once or twice a week is almost inevitably to have to try—

though, alas, not necessarily with success—to make oneself a poet.

For our natural insensibility there is no permanent cure. One may seek new sights and new wonders, but that aid to awareness, like other stimulants, must be used with caution. If the familiar has a way of becoming invisible, the novel has a way of seeming unreal—more like a dream or a picture than an actuality. And certainly no man is less aware of things than the conscientious traveler who hurries from wonder to wonder until nothing less than the opening of the heavens on judgment day would catch the attention of his jaded brain. Madder music and stronger wine pay diminishing returns.

I have never practiced the swami's technique for "heightening consciousness" and I doubt that I ever shall. For one thing, I am not sure that I want to be so exclusively aware of either myself or the All in the colorless essence of either. To put it in a dignified way, I prefer to live under the dome of many-colored glass and to rest content with the general conviction that the white radiance of eternity has something to do with it. To put it more familiarly, what I am after is less to meet God face to face than really to take in a beetle, a frog, or a mountain when I meet one.

My own homely technique when I walk out in my own country and realize that I am in danger of seeing nothing at all is simply to greet each thing as it comes along, by name if I know it: "That is a wood frog," "This is the caterpillar of *Papilio glaucus*," and "This is some member of the Compositae clan I don't remember ever to have seen before." Usually, if the thing is not too common, I stop a moment to pass the time of day with it, much as one does with an acquaintance met on the street. "A nice day—for frogs," I may remark pleasantly; or, perhaps, "I don't think I've seen you since last summer." The plants and animals to whom I issue such bits of conversational small change are not any more interested or impressed than the people to whom one says the same things, but neither are they much less so. And in both cases the purpose achieved is much the same. I have noticed them; sometimes they have noticed me; and I am reminded of something which a certain kind of person is rather prone to forget—that there are other creatures in the world beside himself.

Here, in this new and almost absolutely different country which I am trying somehow to take possession of, the technique requires certain modifications when I stroll casually about my own private eight or ten acres of desert. I am in a world of strangers, none of whom I have ever seen before unless it was very briefly on previous visits, and by no means all of whom I recognize even from books. Under the circumstances, the expected is reassuring. There is no doubt

about the fact that that ridiculous, donkey-eared creature with the long hind legs and the stringy torso is a
jack rabbit; or that the huge, hairy creature who has
just crawled out from under a stone is the so-called
tarantula who got his misnomer from settlers with
some misinformation about the Italian spider whose
poison was supposed to inspire an irresistible desire
to dance—preferably a tarantella. Most people would
find him hard to love or even to admire, but in my
fresh enthusiasm for the new fauna—and fortified as
I am with the assurance of the arachnologist that he is
little inclined to bite and would inflict no very serious
damage if he did—I greet him with enthusiasm as
something expected and recognizable.

No less unmistakable is that broad, flat, spiny lizard whose appearance gives some justification for
calling him a horned toad, and whom I pick up with
confidence because I have been told on good authority that he frequently does not move very fast, that
he is perfectly inoffensive, and that he seems almost
to like to be stroked on the horny back which is quite
soft if rubbed the right way of the spines.

The same authorities, I remember, have also assured me that for once—and just to keep one in the
habit of not rejecting too scornfully the improbable
—a popular belief is quite correct. The horned toad
can and does squirt blood out of his eyes when sufficiently worked up. None of the authorities, however,

has told me why it is that whereas most small lizards have to move so quickly to escape their enemies, the horned toad seems capable of no great speed. Why were not all of his kind gobbled up long ago? I risk a speculation which pleases me, though it is probably wrong. Perhaps it is because his shape, broad and almost circular in outline, makes him inconvenient to swallow. Most of the other little lizards have figures which seem especially designed to facilitate their passage down the gullets of snakes and birds.

Unlike the jack rabbit and the horned toad, the majority of the smaller plants and animals are not known to me, either in person or by reputation. The little black pinacate beetle—a sort of hexapodus skunk—who rears on his front legs and goes "Pop," is so famous a character that I say immediately "I'm glad to meet you; I have often heard you spoken of." At first, on the other hand, I am puzzled by the dead twigs lying on the sand, or even still attached to otherwise living plants, completely encased in a coat of adobe which crumbles in the hand but seems to stand out a sixteenth of an inch from the twig it encloses.

"Termites" I guess vaguely and I am right.

But what on earth are those fuzzy insects, some gray green and some red, hurrying about in considerable numbers? At a distance one would say a spider of some sort, but to look a little more carefully is to

41

see that they have the six legs of the insect. At close range, they look rather like gigantic ants in fur coats and they drive me to my books. There, as I discover, they are called, in popular parlance, "velvet ants" though in actual fact they belong to the not too distantly related wasp family. Indeed, what I have been watching is the wingless female of a parasitic wasp which lays its eggs on other, more respectable, wasps or on unsuspecting beetles, but about whose probably reprehensible habits comparatively little is known. There are, however, few insects who do not do something or other surprising, and the velvet ant is not one of those rare, merely humdrum insects. The male has wings and, in the case of some species at least, he seizes the female at mating time and takes her aloft for a plane ride from which she could not walk home if she wanted to.

Perhaps because life presumably began in hot places, such creatures as the scorpions, lizards, and spiders, who represent ancient ways of life, either survive only in regions still conspicuously warm or at least continue only there to flourish in large, bold forms. Farther north, our spiders are small and inconspicuous, as though they had been able to meet competition in a new world only by fitting themselves into the crevices which a more up-to-date population had overlooked. The wolf spider and the gaudy garden spider are the most imposing we can produce. Nothing comparable to the tarantula, nothing which looks so ancient and so typical of the bad old days, stalks boldly about. One need not be learned in evolution to guess that he was more at home before braininess became so common.

But at least we do have spiders everywhere and a tarantula is obviously a spider. For a real glimpse into an almost vanished world, one should look instead at a scorpion who so obviously has no business lingering into the twentieth century. He is not shaped like a spider and he has too many legs to be an insect. Plainly, he is a discontinued model—still running but very difficult, one imagines, to get spare parts for. His translucent flesh—if scorpions can be said to have flesh—makes him look as though he were made of wax rather than clothed in armor like an insect or in skin like a vertebrate. High over his back he holds the conspicuous thornlike sting which he is ready to throw forward over his head, with surprising speed, into the finger of a human being unwise enough to molest him.

I have seen none of the small, deadly kind, only two inches long. I have, however, seen several of the more dangerous looking but actually less dangerous sort, five inches from tail to claw, who threaten with their harmless pincers while the sting poises quietly to strike. I wonder if they court in the same quaint way as the one Fabre describes for the species found in the hottest and driest parts of southern France. There, after much preliminary waving of claws, the male takes the female by the hand and quietly backs into his burrow, leading her after him. I hope that as he does so he sings the antediluvian equivalent of Don Giovanni's "Lá ci darem la mano," which Zerlina found irresistible.

Though so far, at least, I have not had the privilege of seeing anything of this sort, I did, quite by accident, play Peeping Tom to the wooing of two lizards just outside my window. What I saw was sufficient to suggest that the techniques of courtship have not changed much in recent years. The parties concerned belonged to a common species, with a tail considerably longer than the four- or five-inch body whose ash color would make it almost invisible on the desert floor if it were not for the dark longitudinal bands on the tail held high over the back as the creature skims, with lightning speed, from cactus to cactus. When I first noticed this pair the male had just made a direct, crude approach toward the female and she, quite properly resenting his matter-of-factness, scurried away as from an enemy about to devour her. The male stopped disappointed; shrugged his lizard shoulders; started off in the opposite direction; and was then obviously surprised to discover that he was being followed at a discreet distance. He turned and she fled again—though not so fast or so far—and then the real courtship began.

Besides the advances and retreats which are the essential features of all courtships, this one consisted principally of poetical speeches or amorous arias, though I could not be sure which since the sounds were completely inaudible to me, at least through the window. The male would mount some two-inch elevation, raise himself high on his front legs, inflate his throat until he looked like a small iguana, and then give voice to some sort of utterance which shook his whole body from head to tail. His lady would listen intently, move a little closer, and then edge away again when her suitor approached to ask what effect his eloquence had produced.

The performance went on for some two hours. All courtships are too long for everyone except the participants, and I am sorry to say that I did not see how it ended. I am even sorrier to have to report that it was beginning to look as though the suitor was losing interest though the lady was not.

At any rate, I saw enough to realize that this sort of thing has been going on among the members of the animal kingdom for a very long while indeed and that it is probably too late to try to do anything about it. In this case I hope the ultimate result was some more little lizards to continue one of the most ancient lines. That such a happy event sometimes does occur I know, because I discovered, just about the time of this courtship, several inch-and-a-half long individuals of the same species scampering about in the dry herbage by my patio wall.

This is strangeness enough for one day. With lizards and scorpions at my feet, saguaro and mesquite when I raise my eyes, and bare, patient, eroded mountains on the horizon, I am not likely to find anything too familiar to be noticed. Perhaps, indeed, I shall never again see any of these things quite as completely as I do now at this moment when I have grown just sufficiently accustomed to my new environment to be able to take it in but by no means accustomed enough to take it for granted.

No doubt the time will come, even within my year, when I shall have to remind myself to look; and then, when I have looked, remind myself to see. But that time is not yet. When an Arizona cardinal flashes by my window, I am aware, without needing to tell myself about it, how much more brilliant he is than the southeastern species which occasionally takes up residence in New England. When a white-winged dove calls across the desert, it no longer sounds owl-like or sinister, and it is dovelike because I now know the dove which utters it. But I do still hear it and I still take it in.

This is an ideal sort of awareness, the kind one

would have always if one could. Perhaps, indeed, there are a few individuals who do live continuously with it. But one has some doubts when one notices how regularly even those who most desire it put back into some past the happy time when it was really theirs.

Says Wordsworth:

There was a time when meadow, grove, and stream,
The earth, and every common sight
To me did seem
Apparell'd in celestial light,
The glory and the freshness of a dream.

"*In youth,* before I lost any of my senses," says Thoreau, "I can remember that I was all alive." But in Thoreau's case also, it was "once" and not "now" that he had experienced in simple life joys such "as might inspire the muse of Homer and Shakespeare."

At least, both Wordsworth and Thoreau knew that when the light of common day seemed no more than common it was because of something lacking in them, not because of something lacking in it, and what they asked for was eyes to see a universe they knew was worth seeing. For that reason theirs are the best of all attempts to describe what real awareness consists of, and for an opposite reason Walter Pater's is certainly the fussiest, if not actually the worst. Surely no one ever succeeds for long in burning "with a hard and gemlike flame" if his method is the method recommended by the inventor of that dubious phrase. When he advises us to stalk, as it were, exquisite sensations, and seems to warn us how alert we must be if we are not to miss one of those special moments when something or other in nature, or art, or music is reaching perfection, he talks as though only a few things were worth experiencing. How unlike Wordsworth and Thoreau, who realized that the rare moment is not the moment when there is something worth looking at but the moment when we are capable of seeing.

I shall not delude myself into thinking that at this moment the fauna and flora of the desert are "coming to perfection." I know that if they seem fascinating and beautiful it is because I am ready to look not because they are more ready than always to be looked at. And as a guide to life I like better than Pater's fussiness the hearty exclamation of Yorick:

" 'Lord!', said I, '—What a large volume of adventures may be grasped within this little span of life, by him who interests his heart in everything, and who, having eyes to see what time and chance are perpetually holding out to him as he journeyeth on his way, misses nothing he can *fairly* lay his hands on.' "

Pater was an aesthete and Yorick what is commonly called a sentimentalist. But it may be worth pointing out that the "fairly" which is underscored by the sentimentalist does not appear at all in the prescription of the aesthete. Spying upon the courtship of a lizard certainly comes within the limits defined by that adverb, though I am not sure that "collecting" specimens for a museum would.

# Chapter Four

## How Some Others Live There

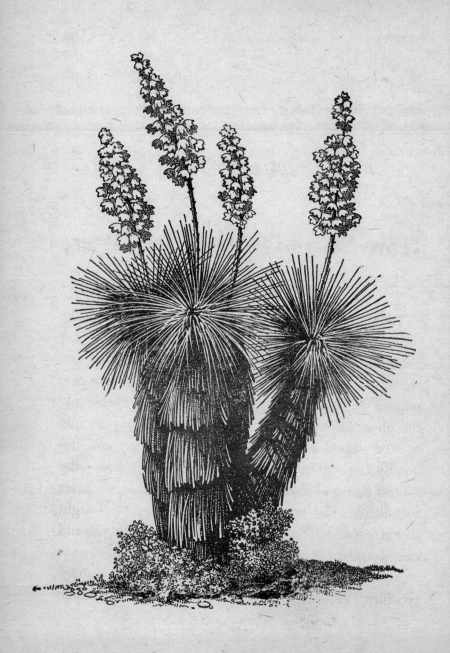

# How Some Others Live There

Today, like yesterday, like the day before, and like the day before that, has been sunny and almost cloudless. The sun has gone down, not, as it sometimes does, riotously and in flame, but leaving behind it in the western sky only a glow which made the clear air seem self-luminous, like the electrically excited gas in a tube. The stars have come out, not one by one, but as though switched on in groups—the largest first and then, group by group, those of lesser magnitude. The wind that has sprung up each night is not cool, but is softly caressing nonetheless and one would have it no different.

No wonder, I said to myself, that certain ancient creatures, no longer fit to live in most other climates, can retire here and never be compelled to know that life elsewhere is hard. Yet for all that, one must not think only of warmth when one thinks of this land. One must think also of that other tremendous fact, dryness; and one must remember that if warmth enables certain old-fashioned creatures to meet here the competition of more efficient organisms as they could not, for example, in New England, drought prevents the fauna as well as, more obviously, the flora, from suggesting what one thinks of as the tropical.

This world, for all its caressing warmth, does not teem. It can be brilliantly colorful but it is never, as a New England summer often is, lush. And like New England at every season except summer, it has its own special kind of austerity, one which has, again like New England, its origin in a climatic severity. Long-continued cold in the one case, long-continued drought in the other, teaches the inhabitants of both regions an art of endurance which gives to each region what many find a part of its charm; and a New Englander might reasonably be expected, for that very reason, to learn more easily to love this land than those native to climates in every way softer could be expected to love it. "Damn braces; bless relaxes" said Blake, and drought and cold are the "damns" which brace, respectively, New England and the Southwest.

In respect to this particular deprivation, the difference between the way in which man and the way in which all other creatures have faced it, is typical. Animals and plants manage to survive on a quantity of water which would soon bring death by thirst to those of any other climate; man, on the other hand, digs wells, channels streams, and in one way or another manages so to modify external nature rather than himself that he uses approximately the same amount of water here as anywhere else.

Six or seven hundred years ago it was just the same. The Indians could not reduce their consumption; in their own cruder ways, they did what the dude rancher around Tucson does—get water rather than do without it. That is no doubt the best way, but when man does fail he fails utterly, as the story of the abandoned cliff dwellings tells so plainly and as, in one of the most recently excavated of them, it is told most plainly of all. Deep wells, up whose vertical sides run steps cut in the earth, still remain. Evidently, as the water became scarcer and scarcer during the great twenty-year drought which afflicted the whole region, the wells were dug deeper and deeper; and one must imagine an unending procession of women climbing up from the depths with pots upon their heads to be emptied onto the rows of corn and squash without which neither women nor men could survive. Finally the heroic enterprise failed. Perhaps, as there is some reason for believing, the victims found refuge with other tribes in less parched regions; perhaps they all perished at last. But in either case they abandoned their homeland to the humbler creatures who had learned, as the Indians had not, the great art of how-to-do-without.

It is an art both the desert plants and the desert animals have learned to practice, but it is the plants' appearance that has been most obviously modified by it. Most of the birds show no outward signs that they live in a land of little rain, and the quail who sit thirty feet up in the saguaro, pecking moisture from its fruit, look, on the ground, as sleek as their cousins who drink when they like. Your rabbits, chipmunks, and other small rodents come in pale desert colors which seem to suggest the dryness of their surroundings, but that is more a matter of protective coloration than the actual result of short rations of water. Almost every plant, on the other hand, has modified itself in some visible way and announces to the most casual beholder that moisture is precious.

One does not need to be much of a botanist to notice that, except for the cactus, most of the plants are merely desert versions of those familiar in other regions. The desert poppy, the desert hackberry, the desert mallow, and the desert verbena are only a few examples of plants whose blossoms announce clearly the groups to which they belong. It is also equally easy to see what they have done to themselves in order to survive happily under unusual conditions, and to observe that the devices found useful by one species are repeated in another.

Perhaps there is no better example of the fact that various of nature's children, like various races of men, have arrived independently at the same solutions of the same problems. Just as the bee, the bat, and the bird each discovered for himself the principles of flight, so the same methods of water conservation have been arrived at by wholly different plant families, each of which has evolved independently of the others. Some anthropologists have argued that the existence in widely separated human tribes of such things as the swastika, the throwing stick, and the bow and arrow prove that the cultures had a common origin. But if animal families can independently invent wings, if plant families independently arrive at succulence and thorns, why should it seem improbable that the phenomenon of convergence could also manifest itself in connection with human ingenuity? Certainly the lines along which the plants have worked are few and they are directed toward three simple ends: to get water, to conserve it, or to get along most of the time without any. Moreover, the few practical devices for achieving any of these ends are repeated over and over again.

To get water, one may of course send roots deep; this, as might be expected, certain trees do, though the method is the more remarkable in certain plants, notably the yucca, whose above-surface size is mod-est. Up the slopes of the gleaming gypsum dunes in White Sands, New Mexico, one may see the yuccas lifting their oddly lush masses of lily blossoms above the burning, bone-dry powder in which it does not seem possible that anything could live and in which, as a matter of fact, precious few other things can. The secret is a root which may, I am told, go forty feet down to the soil below the gypsum.

But how on earth, one may well ask, can a seedling live long enough in a pure, only slightly soluble chem-ical to grow a forty-foot root? The answer to that is another secret. Like the snow drifts which they re-semble, these gypsum dunes shift slowly. In the vales between, the soil is sometimes only a short way down. In some such valley a seedling starts, and then, as the sand drifts over it, the yucca lifts its head higher and higher to keep the air-breathing leaves above the surface. Sometimes, no doubt, it loses the battle and is buried hopelessly in the hot, dry powder. Sometimes, on the other hand, it wins; and then one may see it, triumphantly crowning a mountain of gypsum from which not even the most resourceful plant could draw sustenance.

Sometimes, on the other hand, it is hardly worth while for a plant to go down because there is little water even at forty feet. Hence, the kind of plant which grows in any given desert region depends in considerable part on whether there is water beneath the surface. Ten or fifteen miles north of where I am settled, the yuccas grow everywhere in the loose, rocky soil of a mountainside where there is little earth but where the loose gravel allows water to soak in. Here, on the flat, packed sand, they do not. The saguaro flourishes because its method is not to go deep but to seize quickly and to store up what falls in rare, brief, sudden downpours that run off quickly without penetrating far below the surface. These monster cacti, sometimes as high as fifty feet, sometimes weighing as much as two tons, and sometimes living as long as two hundred years, have no real taproots at all. Just below the surface of the soil, a flat, disk-like network spreads for yards around them; when a rain comes they quickly take up the water from a wide area, swelling visibly and sometimes absorbing as much as a ton of water from one rain. After that they may go a year, if necessary, without taking in water again.

But for the dependence upon this method they do pay one penalty. In the high winds which in summer not infrequently sweep across the desert, as across the sea, they sway visibly, like great trees in the wind; and sometimes, because they are so shallowly rooted, they topple over to lie prostrate for years as whitening skeletons, as hard gaunt ribs from which the flesh has long since rotted away. The common, corpulent barrel cactus of this region, four or five feet high and two or three in girth, evidently roots itself even less securely, for one frequently sees it either completely overturned or leaning crazily—in which latter case it may still bear, as one does at this very minute, its gaudy circlet of waxy, orange-red flowers.

All the methods of keeping water, once one has got it, are variations of the same one, namely, a method of preserving a high ratio of mass to surface. That means thick, succulent leaves (if any); stems which store up moisture, and which also often serve the purpose of leaves—since leaves are too lavish in their evaporation to be afforded by some desert plants. The cactus, of course, is the plant which seems most typical of these devices. Its thick, watery stem bears no leaves at all and, being green all over because of the chlorophyll distributed over its whole surface, the stem can everywhere manufacture the body-building materials which it is the function of the leaves to produce in a normal plant. But in most of the desert plants which do have leaves and which remain green during the dryest seasons, the leaves are at least thick and hence resist evaporation; in the case of the omnipresent creosote bush, they are also coated with a resin which defies evaporation.

Moreover the cactus is·not the only plant which has learned its special trick. It is practiced notably by the paloverde, and is indeed responsible for a part of the charm of that tree. Yet the paloverde is not related to the cactus and must have learned independently that in a land where sunshine for photosynthesis is abundant but moisture is too scarce to be wasted by leaves the clever thing to do is to put chlorophyll into the bark where it may not use sunlight so efficiently—and who cares where there is so much of it—but does save water. In the less arid parts of the year the paloverde, remembering no doubt some ancient habit, puts out small leaves. But when moisture begins to fail, it drops them promptly, exposing merely its network of green twigs to the light. The bean family to which it belongs is totally different from that of the cacti, and no one could possibly mistake one for the other. But they have worked out the same useful methods.

As for the plants which neither send roots deep nor practice conservation so conspicuously, they choose to riot briefly and then lie low, either as seeds waiting for their short weeks of life or, sometimes, as dry roots or shriveled stems hoping for a rainy day. For the most part they are small, like the herbaceous plants of a garden, and they burst suddenly into a riot of blossom. It is they which are chiefly responsible for the desert's sensational spring (which I have never seen), and it must be strangely like that of the arctic, where the shortness of the warm season produces the same result as the shortness of the wet one. In both regions the plants rush from bud to seed with astonishing rapidity. Of the prudence, the foresight, and the thrift of the paloverde or the cactus these desert prodigals seem to know little and care less. *"Carpe diem"* and "We're a long time dead" are their guiding principles. But, like their human analogues, they are responsible for a good deal of the color and gaiety of their world.

Thorns, prickles, and spines are everywhere and, not infrequently, even on the stems or leaves of the short-lived herbs. They represent another device which must have been independently invented many times, and they are no doubt responsible for the fact that, to some, the desert seems an unfriendly place. But the thorns are, after all, defensive devices, necessary, I suppose, because where growth is slow and uncertain the loss of a branch or even a leaf is far more serious than in regions where it can be rapidly replaced.

What Samuel Butler called the "rights of the vegetables" are little respected in New England. The casual walker plucks a flower here, breaks a branch there, and treads down the struggling shrub in his path. In the desert, one walks circumspectly and one thinks twice before seizing even a branch which does not at first sight look spiny. One knows that the rights of the vegetables are being looked after by the only parties likely, in the long run, to look out for anyone's rights—the parties most directly concerned. On the other hand, the little animals who share the desert with these prickly growths have managed very well to adapt themselves. Here and there one sees the armored paddle of a prickly pear half gnawed away by the wood rat who has made his nest among its roots. Many different birds feast off the pulp or seeds of the cactus fruits which a man cannot pluck without disaster to his fingers. In the cholla, fiercest of the cacti, both the cactus wren and the thrasher build their nests.

As for the animals, some of them drink when they get a chance; and I have caught sight of the commonest of the little lizards darting his tongue two or three times into the water of a small ditch dug to irrigate a cultivated shrub. Nevertheless, many of the rodents seldom drink, since they depend largely upon the moisture in the plants they eat. Others never drink at all; and there are a few which never even eat any food not bone-dry. Theirs is the ultimate ingenuity; and one needs to be a chemist to understand how they do it, for without ever taking in any moisture at all they nevertheless give some out and their veins continue to run blood, not sand.

The key to the riddle is the fact that water is composed of hydrogen and oxygen and that these elements, otherwise combined into carbohydrates, exist in the starch of even the dryest seeds the never-drinking rodent eats. In the laboratory of his digestive system he breaks these carbohydrates down, and by recombining two of the elements he makes for him-self the water he must have. For that feat he deserves, I think, to be called the desert dweller par excellence and to rank, as an example of just how far nature will sometimes go, just a little above the boogum tree (*Idria colunaris*) which is certainly the oddest speci-men of desert flora, as he is the oddest of the fauna.

Unlike the rodent which never drinks but is never thirsty, the boogum tree is not really native to the American part of the Sonoran Desert. One finds it wild only in Lower California; nevertheless, it will grow here if planted. If I had not seen it with my own eyes, I should not believe it, for it is far more improb-able looking as a tree than the giraffe is as an animal. Whether it was christened by some admirer of Lewis Carroll or whether some accident of convergence is responsible for the fact that even the gravest botani-cal treatises call it by a name which occurs elsewhere only in *The Hunting of the Snark*, I do not know. In any event, the name is gloriously appropriate because the boogum tree looks far more like something out of *Alice* or the *Snark* than like any real tree.

What one sees when one undertakes to contemplate it is an inverted, green-barked cone, six or eight feet high and with the proportions of a carrot. The general effect is rather like a large taproot that has for some reason grown up into the air instead of down into the earth. From this cone scattered twigs a few inches long project foolishly in all directions. At some seasons a few futile leaves dangle from these twigs, though they were bare when I saw them. Only another Lewis Carroll word will do to describe it; like the borogoves in *Alice*, it is "mimsy"—which, as Humpty-Dumpty explained, means both flimsy and miserable.

So inelegant a solution of a problem is seldom achieved or at least seldom persisted in by Nature, who may not be infallible but who has buried most of her mistakes in geologic time, where this one ought to have been forgotten along with some of the equally inadvisable animals who had their regrettable day. The essayist Charles D. Stewart once analyzed the orthodox tree "as an invention," but he did not mention this one which, so far from being a credit to the inventor, looks like one of those unbelievable triumphs of no ingenuity exhibited by the patent office in hopes of raising a smile. To see three of these vegetable monstrosities together—and three together I have seen, one like a chunky carrot, the other two foolishly elongated—is to suspect that some of nature's journeymen had made trees and not made them well, they imitated an organism so abominably. If the time ever comes when the desert no longer seems to me at all strange, I know how I shall remind myself that it is. I shall imagine a mouse-that-never-drinks resting in the conical shade of a boogum tree.

# *Chapter Five*

# Desert Rain

# Desert Rain

Sometimes it does rain—and hard.

This I always knew but did not really believe. Now, after my first weeks of perpetually cloudless sky, it seemed more improbable than ever. The soil was hard-packed for all its sandiness and bone dry. The cactus and mesquite, standing defiantly under the sun, seemed to survive without moisture. The weather-man, I found myself thinking, must have an easy time here. If he could only content himself with saying "Fair and warmer" every day, he would be bound, statistically, to be right more often than satire credits him with being anywhere else.

The fragments of puffy clouds which one day dotted the sky could not possibly mean anything. Two

69

days later, when a few of them developed black bottoms, that could not mean anything either. And then, twenty-four hours after that, with the sun still pouring down upon me, I rubbed my eyes. Fifteen or twenty miles away, across the still burning desert, a dark veil was descending from a cloud to the mountainside. It could happen there, so why not here? Not to hold the reader in suspense, it did.

In this Lower Sonoran region, the average annual precipitation varies from four inches at Yuma to eleven at Tucson. That means approximately one-tenth to one-fourth of what southern New England gets, and it also means many many more days of drying sunshine. The rain comes mostly during two brief periods, one in midsummer, one in midwinter. And when it does come, it sometimes comes copiously. In some places as much as one-third of the total annual fall has been known to come down in half an hour. Though that is unusual, flooded streets in the city, impassable roads in the country, are normal and expected. A little later, on a trip south to the border, I was to be stopped time and time again by raging, unfordable torrents cutting straight across the unpaved road. Yet, after half an hour, each had shrunk until it was no longer dangerous; after an hour it had disappeared, leaving only a belt of damp sand. These "washes," as they are called here, or "arroyos," as they are called in California, trap both the ignorant and those who have grown contemptuously familiar. That drowning should be one of the commonest fatal accidents in the desert is only another of its paradoxes.

What the winter rains are like I do not yet know, but those of the summer seemed to be invariably accompanied by thunder and prodigious strokes of lightning which, in the distance, crack open the great bowl of the sky from the horizon almost half-way to the zenith. Moreover, as I have discovered, they are very sharply localized. That first descending veil which I saw never reached me, never, as a matter of fact, moved far from where I first saw it. Later, I was to count as many as five completely separate downpours, spaced evenly around half the circumference of the horizon.

Of course, such rains are more common in the surrounding mountains than here on the lower desert plain. The vivid and accurate name which the meteorologists have for such deserts as this is "rain shadow." The mountains, usually wringing the last drop of moisture from the air lifted up over the coldness of their summits, cast an elongated shadow of dryness to the leeward, exactly like the similar though shorter shadow of sunlessness, now to one side and now to the other of their bases. The mountains I see all around me are themselves ordinarily in such a shadow cast by the still higher mountains behind them. What little moisture those higher mountains have failed to extract, these usually take. What we get here is only what they, in their turn, have left. No wonder it is not much, or rather not frequent.

So limited in size are the few laden clouds which manage to survive the double wringing, that torrents may come down here, or in the city a few miles away, while no drop falls on the asphalt or the sand, as the case may be. Permanent residents, weary, as I not yet am, of brilliance and of dryness, grow bitter when they hear that a neighbor got a shower. "It *never* hits where we live."

But they are wrong.

For a week, perhaps, I watched thunderclouds gather and come to nothing; or saw, a few miles away, the lazy unraveling of some patch of nimbus as its moisture dropped slowly to earth. Then one day our time came. The lightning moved closer; the thunder roared in our very ears; and, finally, the huge drops beat down viciously, leaving little craters in the sand where they fell. That time there was not much; but five days later the promise was fulfilled and I understood for the first time why the spinner of the Ancient Mariner's tale took only one short, unadorned sentence to tell of the most important event to occur in the poem. "And when I woke it rained." This was the real thing. Here and there on the uneven ground little puddles collected and stayed there, despite the sun which soon returned in full force, for nearly forty-eight hours. And with almost unbelievable promptitude the desert responded.

This is not, of course, the real season of bloom. Of that I have never seen more than the tail end, when a little red flame is still ascending from the ends of the ocotillos and when, here and there, a few of the humble little plants which will soon dry almost into invisibility are still a mass of brilliant colors. In general, the time of this July rain is the time when plants which have fruits to mature mature them, and those which have not sink into a kind of waiting slumber. "Pears" are reddening or purpling on saguaro and prickly pear, and dry, twisted bean pods on the mesquite. But there are a few things, apparently, which choose this rather than spring as the time to flower, and a few which are stimulated into a second blooming. Desert marigolds appear suddenly in yellow masses of color. White zinnias bloom almost overnight, and on the floor between chollas and paloverdes I notice for the first time a three-lobed vine which I do not know and which has called my attention to itself by bursting out with large, irregular flowers whose yellow throats are delicately lined with purple. More surprisingly, the mesquite and the creosote bush are, for the second time this year, in flower.

But the oddest thing was a tentative sound which I heard first after the first insignificant shower. It came to me from somewhere out of the darkness, plaintive and feebly strident. It could be only some kind of a frog or toad, though no frog I had ever heard offered up to whatever his gods may be a plea like that. I could not remember ever having heard about any desert frogs. Snakes, lizards, and tortoises, of course; but frogs, no. How, in a land where it is almost always dry, could a frog possibly find opportunity to lead that double life signified by the name of the group to which he belongs: the Amphibia. No wonder, I thought, that his voice sounds plaintive. How else can a creature who, so far as I know him, is happy only when wet or at least damp, be anything but plaintive if the great Mother Nature has perversely cast his lot in a sandy waste? No frog of my acquaintance would put up with it.

After the second rain—the real one—the whole desert was suddenly vocal. Frog voices were lifted on every side. One might have thought one was living in a marsh not a desert; might indeed, except for the strange southern accent, have supposed oneself back in New England on some spring day. Yet the songs, though no longer tentative, were nevertheless not the pure jubilation of the peeper. There was still, I fancied, a plaintiveness in them, as from a lingering sense of wrong. "It's high time," they said, "and we oughtn't to have been compelled to wait so long."

I seized a flashlight and went out to investigate.

Being, like all members of their tribe, ventriloquists, they were at first not easy to locate. A voice always retreated as I approached, seemed always to be under the cholla or the clump of mesquite just beyond. At last, however, I came upon a monster puddle perhaps ten feet across and several inches deep. And there they were—some sitting gravely, knee-deep around the margin, others swimming happily about, only their goggle eyes above water but their hind legs visible below the surface as they gave the frog's perfect demonstration of the most effective leg stroke. One old fellow, sitting on the dead, fallen trunk of a cholla just at the water's brim, suddenly inflated his white throat and released a happy cry with an enthusiasm which shook him from stem to stern. I have never heard anything more heartfelt. The plaintiveness was gone, past wrongs were forgotten. He was hailing the wetness as a cock hails the first light of dawn. The swimmers on the other hand were merely practical fellows. Their actions demonstrated that this was the world-as-it-ought-to-be and that they were willing to let it go at that. But the poet had to proclaim it to the world. "Praise God from whom all blessings flow—sooner or later."

The specific name of one of our common eastern frogs is *clamitans*. That, I suppose, is the reason why, in my mind, frogs and the psalmist are all mixed up together. *De profundis clamavi*. It is not, I hasten to add, that I think disrespectfully of the psalmist as an old frog. It is rather that I think of the frog as a psalmist. One calls out from the depths, the other from a puddle. But the God to whom eternity is as a moment may find a similar lack of distinction between what we call depths and what we call puddles. And if the particular frog at whom my flashlight was at the moment pointed was pouring forth thanks rather than appeals for mercy, what he was saying had all the fervor if not all the articulateness of David's, "A merry heart doeth good like a medicine" or "He maketh me to lie down by still waters." The sluggard should go to the ant, but the ungrateful might learn more from a desert frog on a wet night.

No reader, I hope, will mistake my piety for blasphemy. More than one, to my vast amazement, has done so in the past when, for example, I called New England's Day of the Peepers a sort of universal Easter. The trouble is, I suppose, that the pantheist keeps forgetting that his God is not a jealous God and that, since All are One, no part of the whole is offended when another part is praised. He believes in many voices, many prophets, many incarnations, even; and he is grateful for them all. But *revenons à nos grenouilles.*

By the next night all was quiet again. Not one single voice out of what had seemed like myriads was to be heard. It is true that most of the puddles had long since dried up, but not the superpuddle I had investigated. It had shrunk to a quarter of its size, yet it was still bigger than most of those available the previous night and indubitably was still large enough to rejoice half a dozen of the frogs. Nevertheless, not one was to be found. All had vanished as mysteriously as they had come. The desert was again as frogless as I had supposed it always to be.

But why on earth should the creatures have got enough so soon? Must I revise completely my ideas about their tastes and temperaments? Is it possible that they have become so accustomed to an unfroggy dryness that one evening in the water is enough to last them for a while and that they crawl contentedly back to some hole in the sand? How and when do they lay their eggs, and where does that tadpole with which every frog must begin, pass his youth? I know, to be sure, that certain tropical toads have the strange habit of sinking the eggs into little pits on the mother's back where they hatch out in due time and where the tadpoles, never knowing any body of water larger than the few drops which these pits contain, grow up. But if the southwestern frogs (mine, I am beginning to suspect, are actually toads) had any such fantastic habit, I am pretty sure I should have heard of it. The explanation must be simpler.

Before long I shall make a trip to consult some

books and perhaps even some expert at the university who will enlighten me. My neighbors, of course, know nothing about the matter. "Sure, in the summertime you always hear those frogs after a rain. Darn things keep me awake sometimes." But their knowledge and their curiosity stop there. So far as they know (or care), frogs may be generated out of the sand when it gets wet, as the Egyptians thought they were generated out of the mud when the Nile overflowed its banks.

A nice old lady, well-bred and what is called well-educated, once remarked to me in passing that the giant waterbugs one often sees flying about street lights in southern cities were generated by the electric current, and when I expressed some skepticism concerning this novel theory of the origin of life she was ready with a proof. They had never been seen in her town until electricity was brought there. Probably they hadn't, because, though they regularly leave the water, it takes a bright light to attract them in numbers at any one place. I decided not to undertake the old lady's education in either natural history or logic. A hundred years is not long and she was not much more than a century behind the times in believing spontaneous generation possible.

Until I get, in time, to my books or my expert I am not too unhappy to leave things as they are. The pleasures of ignorance—at least when accompanied by curiosity—rival those of knowledge, and I get a certain pleasure in this new country by assuming that it is actually unexplored so that what I find has never been found before. It has been a pleasure to check off one by one the expected things—to see my first horned toad and my first jack rabbit. But it has been an equal pleasure to be surprised by some plant or animal as new to me as though it were new to science.

In the long run I should grow restless and uncomfortable. For a reason which I cannot explain, I like to know that somebody knows, or that at least some book has recorded, quite a bit about every creature I am likely to see. I am not sure that I am not a little troubled by the fact that at least in the remoter parts of the world there are thousands of species of insects not yet named or listed. We are a race of Adams and it is assuredly one of our first duties to give names to the creatures who share our Eden. But for the time being I have still a little wondering to do about those frogs.

The clamorousness of their excitement certainly suggested Love. Nothing else works up either amphibia or men to quite such a pitch of excitement. But the largest of my puddles is not likely to last more than two or three days, and there is no permanent body of water anywhere about. If eggs are laid, even if tadpoles are hatched with most unusual speed, they will certainly perish in the drought. Yet the adults are proof enough that some do somewhere survive. Perhaps pools last longer during the winter rains. Perhaps that is the real breeding season and perhaps what I have witnessed is a sort of second blooming, like that which has come upon the mesquite and the acacia. After all, there are plenty of tadpoles to spare. They are produced only less prolifically than the spermatozoa of the mammals. That the vast majority wriggle for a few hours and then die probably troubles nature no more in one case than in the other.

My frogs have not, I am sure, been allowed to take advantage of the swimming pools—tiled, vacuum-cleaned, and chlorinated—with which estate owners have dotted the desert. But certain other creatures have. And since man has been, on the whole, a curse to nearly every other creature, it is always a pleasure to be able to note that something—like the swallows who use his chimneys and the birds which habitually weave bits of his string into their nests—has been able actually to profit from his presence.

Every evening about sunset considerable companies of bats and night hawks swoop down over the swimming pools to take water on the wing. Probably, there were not so many of them before this artificial water was provided, and probably they would become far less common again if man and his artesian wells were to disappear together. Most people seem to tolerate them, but there is another visitor less complacently accepted—a good-sized yellow wasp with black wings which actually lights on the surface, rests there drinking for several minutes and then, unlike most insects who are lost once they touch the water, takes off again. One man I know has actually gone to the length of adding to his pool one of the new wetting agents, with the result that his visitors drown. I cannot say that I blame him too much, since wasps are not very desirable swimming companions. But I can't help thinking that it must be a shock for a creature who has been accustomed through millions of years to practice its maneuver to discover all at once that water has ceased to have a surface film.

# Chapter Six

# What the Desert Is Good For

# What the Desert Is Good For

Before I settled in the Lower Sonoran Desert I spent a few days in the foothills of New Mexico's Sacramento Mountains. From a height we looked down on Alamogordo and, beyond that, across twenty or thirty miles of white gypsum sand to the forbidden spot where the first atom bomb was exploded.

There must be very few places in the United States so suitable for such an experiment; few, that is to say, either so remote or so devoid of anything to be destroyed. Indeed, anyone sufficiently innocent who had happened to see that phenomenon might have wondered why so much trouble was taken to devastate a region already so thoroughly devastated. Several hundred square miles thereabout look very much as though they had all been worked over not so long ago by some very effective destructive agent; after the bomb had gone off, one might, with some justification, have inscribed over the spot the epitaph which seems a little overwrought for the situation in which Swinburne used it: "As a god self-slain on his own strange altar, Death lies dead."

By now, I imagine, certain forms of life have crept back at least to the edge of the bomb pit itself. Something lives almost everywhere. On the bare rocks of high mountain peaks flourish the lichens which, even some of the more sceptical astronomers now admit, might grow in the atmosphere of the planet Mars. In Wyoming, the stone basins of the scalding hot springs are bright with yellow algae. In the almost saturated brine of the Great Salt Lake, a shrimp which cannot live unless thus dreadfully pickled passes his presumably happy life. And it is in the sandiest parts of the White Sands that the yucca sends down its forty-foot root while pale, sand-colored rodents dig about its base.

I dare say that there is a point, different for different people, beyond which the spareness of difficult countries ceases to be an encouraging example, and a point beyond which the dimmer forms of life awaken but little fellow feeling. Birds are among the least human, one might almost say the least understandable, of the conspicuous creatures of which men are commonly much aware. But there are many persons to whom their beauty and charm would seem a sufficient reason why the universe should exist and who can contemplate without horror a terrestrial globe of which they would be the only significant inhabitants. Not many, however, will follow Thoreau into his professed complacency at the thought that mud turtles would continue to exist even if man should destroy himself; and I doubt that even Thoreau would find emotionally satisfying a world in which nothing lived except lichens and brine shrimp.

A lichen is an admirable organism. It is the first colonizer of bare rock, and it can live where nothing else can. It has, if I may be so impudent as to put it this way, my great respect. Mars seems a trifle less bleak when I think that lichens may grow there. The thought of a dead universe is harder to bear than the thought of one in which green scales expand and grow a little before they die. But they would seem a rather small favor to be grateful for, and I can hardly maintain that my respect is anything much warmer than just that.

What I like, for a time at least, about this particular spot where I have settled is the fact that it is just far enough—without being too far—from the point beyond which spareness would cease to be stimulating and the life of my fellow inhabitants too desperately precarious. On the one hand, it is a very proper environment for those, including myself, who like it. On the other, it is not crowded either with men or with any other form of life. And for those who dislike crowds of anything, that is a strong point in its favor. The land simply will not support either too many people or too many mesquite trees. Hence, we both have room.

I grant that in many places nature herself seems to have set man the example for his strange conviction that the number of individuals of every species ought to be multiplied until that point is reached where they kill one another off in one way or another. That is one way of putting the Malthusian law, whose most regrettable feature is the second preposition in the phrase "up to and *beyond*" the food supply. I grant further that this law operates in the desert as it does everywhere else and that if we are not crowded here it is not because the human, the animal, or even the vegetable communities have exhibited a superior wisdom. It is merely because, for all of us, the limit is sooner reached. Nevertheless, I cannot help seeing as an advantage the simple fact that the land here is dry enough to prevent uncomfortable crowding, and I cannot help wondering if one of the worst features of most of the world in which we live is not the simple fact that, to an ever increasing degree, mere living space is the thing which gives out first.

It is a commonplace that man's ingenuity has made it possible for the earth to support many times the number of men that could possibly live on it were it not for our advanced techniques of agriculture and manufacturing. I can understand why in times past, when men found themselves too few and too scattered for comfort or security, an increasing population should have seemed desirable. But is it really an encouraging rather than a terrifying fact that biochemists are already beginning to talk seriously of producing in yeast vats a protein food capable of supporting a population far larger than has ever seemed possible before? Where (and how) will the billions more who can possibly be fed, find places to live? Will vast tenements go up on the corn and wheat fields which will no longer be necessary? Will every square foot of soil ultimately be not only owned but occupied? Will every other living thing be exterminated to make way for the one vast anthill of yeast-eating men? Even then, the limit would be reached at last. Would it not be better to reach it while we still have a little room to move about? I, at least, shall probably continue to think so unless some scientist can tell me not only how to produce more food but how to open up the fourth dimension for elbowroom.

Of the president of a certain agricultural college on his first trip to Europe, this story is told. He was leaning pensively over the ship's rail when he was offered a penny for his thoughts. Waving his arm over the vasty deep which has touched the imagination more often and deeply than anything else in nature except, perhaps, the starry heavens, he replied: "You know, I was just thinking what a pity it is that all this can't be put down in alfalfa." There are, no doubt, others who never see a bird without thinking of the pot, or a wood without leaping happily forward to the day when it will make newsprint, and who never observe any stretch of wild open country without wishing it were covered with skyscrapers or factories or bungalows. More souls for heaven? They will be, I think, ill-prepared for it.

Is there really any virtue in mere numbers—even of men? The biblical injunction "Increase and multiply" was given to a struggling tribe more in danger of extinction than of overcrowding, and undoubtedly there is some optimum concentration below which the most effective cooperation and division of labor is not possible. It may even be true that centers, over-populated for any other purpose, perform an indispensible function; I should hesitate to say that I, as an individual, would like to dispense with what I have learned in some of them. But in such places there is also much that is unlearned and much forgotten. When there has disappeared from the earth the last spot, even the last accessible spot, where something besides man and his immediate dependents holds sway, then mankind will have renounced utterly its ancient mother and will be arrogantly on its own. But for what will man have condemned himself to so impoverished an existence? For nothing except a more numerous breed.

It is hard to ask ourselves whether and why numbers alone should seem desirable, hard to dissociate our hope that we love mankind from the assumption that such love necessarily means a limitless desire for more and more specimens. But Thoreau was one of the few who actually did face the dilemma and who frankly stated his conclusions. Visiting New York at twenty-six, he wrote: "Seeing so many people from day to day, one comes to have less respect for flesh and bones, and thinks they must be more loosely joined, of less firm fiber, than the few he had known. It must have a very bad influence on children to see so many many human beings at once,—mere herds of men." Or, as he was later to say, "It is for want of a man that there are so many men." And who that realizes how much the world's respect for the individual has declined since Thoreau's day can be sure that men do not seem less valuable just because there are so many more of them? Men permit themselves to drown kittens because there is no danger that kittens will not be produced in superabundant numbers. The horrible slaughter of whole races may have been tolerated by their conquerors for the same reason.

In any event, there is as yet no crowding of the Sonoran Desert and there is not likely to be any for some time to come—even without the intervention of any such device as that demonstrated at Alamogordo. Through the centuries the development of transportation and industry have made it less and less necessary that a region be directly self-supporting, and perhaps there is no really logical reason why vast stretches of this country should not be "redeemed" from saguaro and doves so that they could be "used" for factories. Perhaps someday, indeed, that will happen. But there is sometimes a happy lag in the progress of Progress, and because the main lines of transportation were laid down in an earlier day, when agriculture was more nearly pre-eminent, the factories will not go up here quite as rapidly as they have elsewhere until the space available nearer established railroads and waterways has been used up. Probably the ax will be laid to our last remaining deciduous forests before the saguaros are felled.

Meanwhile, man has not here utterly upset the balance of nature, and that balance establishes itself at a level of low density for plants, for animals, and for men. Water gives out before anything else does, long before there is simply no more room, and the human population, no matter what its own immoderate impulses may be, is inevitably spread as thin as the desert flowers. Chambers of commerce in the larger cities may dream of more and more irrigation and of more and more industry; but the water will go only so far, even with the mountain dams and the long canals, and the demand for living space will have to be frustrated in other, more easily over-exploitable regions before the dreams of the boosters are realized as the nightmares such dreams have a way of turning into.

Not far from where I am there is a good deal of "cattle country," but the innocent eastern visitor who sometimes wonders, even in much more heavily grazed Texas, where the cattle are, would never suppose that here there were any at all. Just the other day a ranch of fifty-five thousand acres changed hands in my neighborhood, but with the normal allotment in this area of sixty acres per steer the traveler may pass straight through the middle of such a ranch without realizing that the country is being used by man for any purpose whatsoever.

To many who are accustomed to teeming lands all this may make the desert seem niggardly, but to some others her balance soon comes to seem as normal as any other. There is no absolute standard by which one may determine just how many plants, how many cattle, or how many men an acre should support, and there is much to be said in favor of elbowroom.

The way of the desert and the way of the jungle represent the two opposite methods of reaching stability at two extremes of density. In the jungle there is plenty of everything life needs except mere space, and it is not for the want of anything else that individuals die or that races have any limit set to their proliferation. Everything is on top of everything else; there is no cranny which is not both occupied and disputed. At every moment, war to the death rages fiercely. The place left vacant by any creature that dies is seized almost instantly by another, and life seems to suffer from nothing except too favorable an environment. In the desert, on the other hand, it is the environment itself which serves as the limiting factor. To some extent the struggle of creature against creature is mitigated, though it is of course not abolished even in the vegetable kingdom. For the plant which in the one place would be strangled to death by its neighbor dies a thirsty seedling in the desert because that same neighbor has drawn the scant moisture from the spot of earth out of which it was attempting to spring.

Sometimes it seems to me that, of the two methods,

the desert's is the kindlier and that, though I have never seen the jungle, it is there rather than here that I should feel the sense of discomfort (or worse) which the desert produces in some of those who experience it for the first time. Certainly I am little aware of any such discomfort. I wonder if it does not augur ill for the human race that its techniques have enabled it to produce for itself a sort of artificial, technological jungle in which too many people can live somehow—if not well—and where, therefore, as in the jungle, the struggle inevitably becomes ultimately the struggle of man against man and not the struggle of man against nature.

Only recently, I think, has man begun to realize even dimly the extent to which this is true. No doubt the industrial revolution marked the effective turning point. Perhaps, indeed, that revolution might be defined as the sum of the processes by means of which the human race escaped dramatically and almost in a single bound from the limit set to its multiplication by natural conditions and entered upon the period when it began to live in the jungle rather than in the desert. To some extent, of course, every improvement in the methods of agriculture or technology—from the invention of the cooking pot to the invention of the plow or even to the invention of agriculture itself— had tended in the same direction. But for thousands of years such improvements had been slow, and the changes which they brought about moderate. Perhaps, indeed, it was about a century or two ago that the optimum density was reached. And perhaps we are only now beginning to feel the effects of having recently passed it. There are few moralists discussing the world today who do not, sooner or later, get around to the observation that private individuals and governments alike seem to be reverting more and more to what they call, in a rather stale metaphor, "the law of the jungle." Possibly that is less of a metaphor than they commonly suppose.

As I look out of my window here, there is nothing junglelike about what I see. The mesquite and the paloverde trees have arranged themselves as in an orchard; the saguaros stand sentinel, three or four to an acre. Though two or three roofs are just visible above the desert growth, the peaks of the Santa Catalina Mountains, hardly more than a mile away, close the horizon with stone slopes thinly clad in a dark green which at this distance looks more like moss or lichen than like the scattered shrubs which have found there a precarious foothold. It is hard to believe that anywhere else there is overcrowding, that in some sections of New York, for example, those crowded into the skyscrapers would trample one another to death if they tried to reach the ground simultaneously.

In all this, perhaps, is implied a hint of some part of the answer to the question of what I came here to find. Perhaps I laughed to see such quantities of sand partly because sand is room; and room is becoming one of the scarcest things on earth for most people because it is one of the things which no economy of abundance seem to plan to supply abundantly. Even those to whom the desire "to get away from people" seems evidence of some ultimate wickedness may possibly be willing to grant that to want to get away from too many people is innocent enough.

# Chapter Seven

# The Contemplative Toad

# The Contemplative Toad

Those toads who surprised me by coming from
nowhere after our first big rain and who sang their
hallelujah chorus on every side have surprised me
again. They have disappeared as mysteriously as
they came. The desert floor and the desert air are as
toadless as ever. Obviously, they are creatures as
moderate as all amphibia should be, and one night
of revelry was enough.

The next evening I did, to be sure, hear a few scattered voices, like those of stubborn guests who won't
go home when a party is over. But all the rest had
lapsed into silence and retired into invisibility. More
than a month has passed, and despite one more rain
as heavy as that which summoned them forth, not

one has made himself heard. Nevertheless, I have a very good way of knowing that I did not dream the night they took over.

Forty-eight hours afterward, the largest of my puddles was swarming with tadpoles quite unaware of the fact that fate had assigned them an impossible situation. One more day of hot sun and the puddle was only a damp spot in the sand, covered at its very center with a mass of what had once been potential toads. Obviously the tadpoles had drawn closer and closer together as the puddle shrank, much as a human community might have concentrated itself as the waters of some rising flood drove all its members to the last remaining area of high ground. And they had been overwhelmed at last by the suffocating air, as human beings might have been by relentless water.

But how on earth do any ever survive to carry on the population which is obviously in quite a flourishing state? This puddle was an unusually large one. So far as I know, there was no other larger (and there is certainly no permanent water) within a mile or two of its position. I took it for granted that the tadpoles of this particular species must turn into toads in a remarkably brief period. But however brief it might be, it was obviously not brief enough to be covered by my puddle's duration. These toads, it would appear, ought to have become extinct in this region long ago. Obviously, they haven't.

Before long, I found that my ignorance was ceasing to be a pleasure. The first thing I discovered was that I need not have determined—as originally I did —to preserve it for a while; it has turned out to be not easy to dispel. My confidence that of course someone could answer all my questions was faith misplaced. No one, it now appears, knows very much more about my toads than I do.

Fortunately, I captured one of the two-inch adults and I kept him prisoner until I could consult Wright and Wright's authoritative check list of American toads and frogs. It was easy enough to identify him as the Sonoran spadefoot (*Scaphiopus couchii*) who inhabits Arizona, Utah, Mexico, and parts of Texas. He has an eastern relative, not especially uncommon but seldom recognized by the layman. Like all the spadefoots, he is a great digger with his hind legs and he is conveniently distinguished from all the Bufos (the genus to which the common garden toad belongs) by the fact that the contracted pupil of his eye is vertical like a cat's, not round or horizontal like that of the Bufos.

There is, then, no trouble about naming him, but the available information does not go much beyond that. He is believed to mate only once a year and al-

ways after a summer rain. At other periods he has
been accidentally dug up out of the earth. But in
what sort of pool does he successfully raise his family? How much of the time does he remain buried?
Does he come out to eat occasionally during the almost year-long period when he is rarely if ever seen?
Finally, how does he like the extraordinary existence
which he seems to lead? On these questions, the books
cover their silence with the air of not having the space
to go in for that sort of thing. Queried face to face,
the authorities shrug their shoulders: "Wish I knew."

Now, this situation offers a splendid opportunity
for the favorite employment of the amateur in any
field—namely, expert-baiting. Having been myself
sometimes taken for an expert in fields far removed
from the present, I know a great deal about the subject and how the occasions arise. To begin with, all
laymen are stubbornly incurious about the thousand
and one things you could tell them. All that is
pedantry and they are bored. "Who cares?" is their
chronic attitude. And then one morning the telephone
rings and a voice introduces itself by saying "I have
been told that you are an expert on. . . ."

This statement is made in a voice which plainly
implies that the speaker believes himself to have been
imposed upon by an unjustified reputation, and the
form of the introductory remark is intended not to

compliment you by acknowledging your expertness but to make sure of one thing. If you *can* answer the question, it is little to your credit since you pose as an expert and ought to know what is being asked even if you don't know anything else. If you cannot answer promptly, positively, and fully, then you ought to be ashamed of yourself since you are obviously a fraud. "Did they, in the eighteenth century, have an intermission between each of the conventional five acts of a play?" "What was the color of Dr. Johnson's eyes?"

To the first of these questions I think I have found the answer. Nobody—I think—knows the answer to the second, for Johnson squinted, and the best portraits are rather noncommittal. But I have been compelled often enough to disappoint the eager inquirer not to suppose that any biologist ought to feel disgraced because he does not know how a Sonoran spadefoot spends his time. There are so many things that might be known about the hundreds of thousands of creatures sharing this earth with us. And biologists are not exempt from the truth that life is short.

There is a tale, long current in academic circles, about an indolent student who took a course in "The Bible" because it was reported to be a cinch. He attended class infrequently and because he had been told that the only question ever asked on the final examination was "Give a list of the kings of Israel" he spent a night with a towel wrapped around his head learning the list. Next day he was outraged to be faced with only a single sentence on the blackboard. "Criticize the acts of Moses." Not one act could he remember, good, bad, or indifferent. And so, after due thought, he wrote: "Far be it from me, humble as I am, to criticize the acts of the great Moses. But if you would like a list of the kings of Israel *with their dates*, it follows." Not infrequently, I have met that sort of response from experts. Not less frequently, I myself have given it.

But if one *were* going to bait the biologists (which of course I am not), the line of attack would go something like this: Biologists spend too much time in laboratories—which is a highly reputable occupation —and too little observing creatures who are not specimens but free citizens of their own world. The odor which clings to these scientists is too seldom that of the open air, too often that biologist's odor of sancity, formaldehyde. They learn an enormous number of the things which can be learned in a laboratory, especially the things which can be learned by dissecting preserved corpses, but comparatively few of the things which it would take a much longer time to find out in the field.

If, for example, you should want to know just what is the difference between a toad and a frog and if, perhaps, you have some vague sort of idea that one spends more time in the water than the other, or that toads are the kind that have (and give) warts, you will promptly be set right. "A toad is a tailless amphibian having a divided sternum, the cartilaginous element of one side overlapping the other; a frog is a tailless amphibian whose sternum is otherwise." Better yet, if all you want is a name, you will either get it or (most improbably unless you have been traveling in some very remote place) you will become famous in very limited circles as the discoverer of a new species, which may even be called Somethingor-other smithii after you. But if you want to know more than a name, you may very easily run into difficulty. There are thousands of creatures, some of them quite common in well-frequented places, which are *Nomen et praeterea nihil.*

Names are important, of course, and it is worth while to make a good deal of fuss over them because otherwise two observers would not know whether or not they were talking about the same creature, and endless confusion would result. But it is a great pity that all information—and, too often, all curiosity —should stop with what is really only a preparation for learning something. Any biologist whose field of interest includes the amphibia would recognize my toad at a glance. Even a rank amateur like myself can, thanks to the care with which keys to the species have been worked out, find his name without difficulty. He is even rather readily distinguished from a very similar species common in the same region and called *Scaphiopus hammondii*. But very little is known about the lives of either one of them.

At least since the time of Thoreau, amateurs of natural history have been grumbling about this state of affairs. Thoreau himself, when he got hold of a large and costly monograph on the turtle, was outraged to find that in the whole volume not one word was said about how any turtle conducted his life. Since Thoreau's time, a great deal has been discovered and published concerning the sort of thing which he wanted to know about his fellow creatures. But a century after my time others will probably be complaining, as I am now complaining (mildly) a century after Thoreau's.

That is partly because the distinguishing of species is a relatively easy as well as a rather gratifyingly esoteric business. Any young beginner in academic circles who demonstrates to his colleagues that the members of an accepted species can be divided into two slightly different species gets a very conspicuous good mark against his name. In many cases he even helps along a colleague who, a decade later, will again reduce the two species to one, and get an equally good mark against his. Usually, when further study of a carefully named creature is taken up, the next thing to be investigated is the details of his anatomy—simply because that also can be done in a laboratory and from thoroughly dead specimens. Moreover, since most college teachers have been trained in this sort of thing, the introductory college course almost invariably begins not with the observation of some living creature—and it is certainly only because they were once alive that the dead ones are interesting—but with the dissection of a preserved but still smelly earthworm or frog. It is as though the subject of the course were not, as the catalogues maintain, *bio*logy but rather *thanato*logy instead.

Since I am, by trade, a Professor myself, it hardly becomes me to indulge in contemptuous remarks about "the professors," but a certain amount of it is almost obligatory in a book of this sort. Having discharged the obligation, I shall conclude with one concession and one admission. The concession is that the most important reason why there are so many gaps in the available life histories of even the commoner animals is less the perversity of professors than the fact that there are an awful lot of these common creatures and that actually to follow their lives from day to day is a very difficult, time-consuming task. The admission is that, despite my special interest, the definitive monograph on the life history of *Scaphiopus couchii* will not be written by me.

Certain face-saving things I have, however, undertaken to do. Before disappearing among the bound volumes of *Copeia* and the other technical journals in the library of the University of Arizona, I rescued about a score of the tadpoles from the pool to which a careless Mother Nature had unkindly consigned them. Only later did I discover that in Wright and Wright these tadpoles are said to be, unlike other tadpoles of my acquaintance, carnivorous. Perhaps by preference they are. But mine got such green algae as I could lay hands on, plus wheat germ, now so favorably known as a health food. They ate both eagerly, and they not only thrived but beat by four days an official record—transforming themselves into toads in eleven instead of the official minimum of fifteen days.

The first signs of leg buds had appeared in seven days. Forty-eight hours later these legs were functioning, and two days after that the toads left the water. This all but incredible speed of transformation, so fast indeed that one could all but see the body completely reshaping itself while, in the little insides, the vital organs were at the same time changing over from a water- to an air-breathing mechanism, is obviously the explanation of a part of the mystery. These toads can breed in the desert because instead of requiring water, as most frog and toad tadpoles do, for a period running from three months to two years, they require it for only the short time that at least some rain pools must last.

Mine climbed out of the water into which I had put them, still carrying behind them tails of scarcely reduced size. In the course of twenty-four hours these tails shrank to stubs, like the tail remnant of a fox-terrier, and only rarely, perhaps only by accident, did the toads ever get back even briefly into the water I kept available. Yet, rapid as the transformation was it was not rapid enough to permit the survival of those I had left where nature put them. *Scaphiopus couchii* doesn't ask for much. But like exceptionally modest men, he sometimes doesn't get even the little he thinks he could do with.

The technical journals didn't yield much. Seven or eight years ago, a biologist living in Tucson had noted the sudden appearance and sudden disappearance of my friend the Sonoran spadefoot fifteen or twenty miles from where I observed him—about two weeks earlier in the season and under almost exactly the same conditions. But he did not raise any tadpoles and I have no local check on the time I established for transformation. Most of the other references were from somewhat less arid parts of *Scaphiopus'* range and they offered little more than guesses that he breeds but once a year—in midsummer—and that he spends most of the rest of his time buried in the sand.

The only biologist whom I could find sweating out the Summer Session at the University was a specialist in fishes to whom frogs were a matter of considerable indifference. He gave me the address of Dr. Hock, the faculty member who would know most about the subject but who had gone to Alaska—not, as I supposed, merely to get away from frogs for a while but, as it turned out, to become director of a health research center. In any event, I brashly wrote him by air mail, got back a generous letter which had evidently cost him some time, and also the advice to wait for Dr. Lowe, the new herpetologist who was to take his place at the University.

Dr. Lowe greeted me more cordially than, I'm afraid, I always greet those who come to my office in New York to ask whether or not it is all right for them to say "It is me" when answering an intimate friend. He told me some things, politely wished he knew the answers to some other questions, and expressed some interest in my observations on my spadefoot pets. There is even the dizzy possibility that with persistence, luck, and Dr. Lowe's advice, I might some day get five or six lines in *Copeia*. Anyone who has had the experience knows that there is nothing so gratifying as the tiniest recognition outside one's own field. Perhaps, even, I may be able to experience again something like one of the proudest moments of my life. It occurred fifteen years or more

ago when a gentleman to whom I was being introduced asked me if I was, by any chance, the person
of my name who had written, a year or two
previously, an article in *Aquatic Life* with the title
"A Successful Caesarian Operation on a Guppy."

Meanwhile the toadlets to whom I, not nature,
played the tender mother have been leading artificial
but perhaps not unpleasant lives. In the rough world
they would, I presume, have been compelled before
now to take refuge underground, at least from time
to time. But since I did not know just how soon they
would be prepared to endure such desiccation and
since I was anxious not to lose them, they have been
protected against all rigors. The sand on the bottom
of the box to which they have been confined has been
slightly sprinkled daily. Theirs is a world where it
showers pleasantly every afternoon and where food
appears at regular intervals rather than when some
luckless bug happens to wander by. They have been
given such small insects as I could find, plus bits of
meat—waved in front of them on the end of a tooth-
pick—which the more up-and-coming have learned
to take, though the stubborner or the stupider will
have none of it. They have grown prodigiously and it
is worth noting just how high the percentage of viabil-
ity is under favorable conditions. Of the seventeen
original tadpoles, not one failed to become a toad.

Of the four toads I kept, only one failed to survive for at least the two months I tended them all in their box. Obviously, were nature as kind as I, the earth would soon be knee-deep in toads.

Most of them I released to make their own way in the world, taking care only to place them in what looked to me like a good place for creatures of their kind. I have decided to keep indefinitely only one—partly to reduce the trouble of feeding, partly because he or she is to change his status from that of a specimen to that of a pet and it is a bad plan to spread affection too thin. I have bestowed a name—Ina, in honor of the road near which the original puddle collected—and thus I have determined that, whatever anatomy may say, my toad is, by human convention, a she.

All her brothers and sisters had the habit of digging little resting pits for themselves in the damp sand, and once or twice an individual buried himself completely. After their numbers had been reduced, a favorite refuge for those who remained was the narrow crevice between the sand and the edge of a water saucer in which they exhibited otherwise little interest. The daily shower usually brought them out, but most of the time they just sat.

At the present moment, Ina is, as usual, resting—though I don't know from what—in a little cup which her body exactly fits. Her body long ago assumed perfectly the shape of a toad, which is a shape not without dignity and charm if one is broad-minded enough to accept it. She measures well over an inch from the tip of her nose to the place where her tail would be had she cared to keep it. And since the tadpole from which she developed was only one-fifth of an inch, exclusive of tail, I calculate that she has increased her weight one hundred and twenty-five fold; which is as though a human baby were to reach eight hundred pounds in a similar period.

Last night she had raw spareribs for dinner and seemed to find it a tasty dish. But of course I don't know what effect an unusual and probably unusually plentiful diet, as well as other artificial conditions, have had upon her growth. Indeed, I know very little about what her history would have been had she been leading the normal life of her species. And that, of course, is the trouble with laboratory specimens, to say nothing of pets like Ina.

Had I so much as aspired clumsily to science, I should have divided my seventeen baby toads into groups, tried to find out how soon each could endure a given degree of desiccation, what they would do if food was denied them, etc., etc. Even then, to be sure, it would still have been no satisfactory substitute for an attempt to live with the toads in the field, at least as far as that is humanly possible. Going to an opposite extreme, I made a pet of Ina; I am probably oversolicitous of her comfort; and letting science go hang, I grumble mildly at "the professors" for not having found out for me what I am not taking the trouble to learn even as well as I might.

For all I know, Ina may not like the pampering she gets. I can hardly believe that she objects to confinement, for she seldom moves over the fairly generous space allotted her. But perhaps she objects to being kept so continuously warm, damp, and therefore awake. Perhaps she is sleepy; perhaps she is longing to cover her head and sink into some sort of passivity, by comparison with which the four or five hops a day which at present she takes are frenetic. Perhaps she is sick of the sight of food and wishes it were not dangled so frequently before her eyes in such a way as to make it impossible for her to inhibit the reflex which forces her to dart forth a tongue to take it. For all I know, I may be making a Strasbourg goose out of my toad.

In all fairness to myself I must say that she does not look unhappy, only—like all the toad kind—serious, introverted, plunged into Buddhistic meditation. And whether she is happy or not, the details, at least, of the mystery of the desert spadefoots are as mysterious as ever. What on earth do they do with themselves during that nearly year-long period when they seldom, if ever, leave their burrows? Dr. Lowe thinks they may leave them for short periods to feed. He is sure that they are not in that state of suspended animation which the layman thinks of when he hears the word "hibernation." Toads and frogs, he tells me, are always as much alive as the temperature which their bodies have taken on from their surroundings permits. But what a life the Sonoran spadefoot's must be! What does he *do*, buried in the sand for perhaps four-fifths of his time, even allowing for the supposition that he does venture forth to eat?

Gilbert White made famous the ancient tortoise in his garden who spent in naps most of the time he was not officially sleeping his winter sleep. It was, White thought, an odd whim on the part of God to bestow so long a life on a creature who seemed to care so little for it. But the case of the Sonoran spadefoot seems at least as remarkable. Many creatures hibernate and not a few estivate; but he is the only one of my acquaintance who does both, and his condition calls to mind that of the hillbilly of legend who suffered from insomnia. "I sleep fine nights; I sleep pretty well mornings; but in the afternoon I gets kinda restless." Yet on that rainy night when he did wake up, the spadefoot seemed very wide awake indeed.

I sincerely hope that in his underground cell he suffers no touch of claustrophobia. Perhaps this is Hamlet's nutshell and perhaps my toad feels himself, as Hamlet thought he would feel, "king of infinite space." I hope that it is not for him only one long morning-after, spent in recovering from his one big night; and if he meditates, I hope it is not exclusively and liquorishly of some July eleventh, or twelfth, or thirteenth.

Few creatures, surely, have ever been assigned by nature to a life more suited to contemplation. Spadefoots can have little experience of the outside world and hence little material on which to base any conclusions concerning nature or society. But there are subjects for which no experience is necessary. Some think that music, at least in its purely formal as opposed to its expressive aspects, is one. Less disputably, mathematics requires no experience of the world. Presumably a prisoner brought up in solitary confinement all his life might have developed the Pythagorean theorem or even invented Cartesian geometry. If the spadefoots are as thoughtful as they look, they must be engaged with some great abstract question to the pondering of which solitude and immobility are conducive. Perhaps it is something like the possible reconciliation of fate with free will. Or perhaps it is the real significance of the square root of minus one.

I rather hope it is the last, for I have never been satisfied that the practical use of the symbol for it as a direction indicator is the real, or at least the only logical, meaning. Someday, after Ina has had a little more time to think, I am going to whisper suddenly in her ear "Complex variable!" The experiment will be as sensible as some I have read about.

# Chapter Eight

# From a Mountaintop

# From a Mountaintop

In the legends of the saints and the prophets, either a desert or a mountain is pretty sure to figure. It is usually in the middle of one or on the top of the other that the vision comes or the test is met. To give their message to the world they come down or come out, but it is almost invariably in a solitude, either high or dry, that it is first revealed.

Moses and Zoroaster climbed up; Buddha sat down; Mohammed fled. Each in his own way had to separate himself from men before he could discover what it was that he had to say to mankind. In a "wilderness" (Near Eastern and therefore certainly xeric) Jesus prepared himself for the mountaintop from which he would reject the world which Satan would offer. Loneliness is essential and loneliness, it would seem, is loneliest where the air is either thin or dry and nature herself does not riot too luxuriously. If Plato was satisfied with no more than a grove in Athens, that was because he was already halfway to the mere college professor.

Yesterday, when I stood on a peak and looked down at an arid emptiness, I felt on my shoulders an awful responsibility. Under such circumstances as these, said I to myself, other men have grown wise. Only a few before me have ever had the double advantage of mountain and desert. It is now or never. If THE ANSWER is ever to be whispered into my willing ear, this should be the moment.

No awful presence—I hasten to add—handed me any tablets of the law. Neither did Satan appear to offer me the world, and if he had done so I might, for all I can really know, have taken him up. Yet it did seem that I saw something with unusual clearness and that I came down not quite empty-handed.

From where I stood there was no visible evidence that the earth was inhabited. Like some astronomer peering through a telescope at the planet Mars, I could only say, "It might be." It was thus the world must have looked at the end of the fifth day, and I found myself wondering whether the text of Genesis might not possibly be garbled; whether, perchance, it was really after the fifth, not after the sixth day, that God looked at his work and saw that it was good. Would not I, in His place, have stopped right there? Would I have risked the addition of a disturbing element? Was the world ever again so obviously good?

But God's decisions are, by definition, wise, and presumably He knew what He was doing. Perhaps, as some have fancied, He wanted one more projection of Himself to contemplate. Perhaps, as the deists supposed, man is an essential link in that Great Chain of Being which stretches unbroken from the most imperfect up to perfection itself. But in any event, here we are! And here, too, are others, sometimes exasperatingly like us, sometimes exasperatingly different. With ourselves and with these others we must somehow deal.

If one could stay on the mountaintop there would be no problem. To be wise there would be easy. Poetry and philosophy, self-generated, would suffice. But for reasons psychological as well as physical, that we cannot do. Sooner or later we must come down and mingle more or less intimately with populations more or less dense. Men we must meet, and when we meet them we meet Problems. The wisdom found on the mountaintop is not a sufficient guide in the populous lowlands. We must reckon with something which, up there, existed only in the mind or the memory.

But if wisdom, complete and adequate, cannot be brought down, there is something which can and that something is to be found nowhere else. Only from such distance can man be seen either in perspective or in his real context, and it is the absence of that context which invalidates all the solutions to human problems formulated—as today all such solutions are —in no context except that of men's own making. Without this perspective and this context, philosophy and religion degenerate into sociology; and sociology is merely a modern substitute for wisdom. What it lacks is not merely the context of nature, indispensible as that is. It lacks also the context of human nature itself, for which it tries foolishly to substitute some mere observations of human behavior. It calls itself the science of Man, but it has forgotten to ask what Man is really like. The sociologist leaves himself out (he calls this "objectivity") and therefore he leaves out the only thing which would give him a clue to the rest.

Not to have known—as most men have not—either the mountain or the desert is not to have known one's self. Not to have known one's self is to have known no one, and to have known no one makes it relatively easy to suppose, as sociology commonly does, that the central problems are the problems of technology and politics. It makes it possible to believe that if the world has gone wrong—and seems likely to go wronger—that is only because production and distribution are out of balance or the proper exercise of the franchise has not yet been developed; that a different tax structure or even, God save the mark, the abolition of the poll tax in Alabama, point the way to Utopia. It is to forget too easily that the question of the Good Life—both the question what it is and the question how it can be found—has to do, first of all, not with human institutions but with the human being himself; that what one needs to ask first is not "What is a just social order?" or, "In what does true democracy consist?" but "What is Man?".

That question neither the usual politician, nor the usual economist, nor the usual scientist has ever asked, because he has never been alone. No man in the middle of a desert or on top of a mountain ever fell victim to the delusion that he himself was nothing except the product of social forces, that all he needed was a proper orientation in his economic group, or that production per man hour was a true index of happiness. No such man, if he permitted himself to think at all, ever thought anything except that consciousness was the grandest of all facts and that no good life for either the individual or a group was possible on any other assumption. No man in such a position ever doubted that he himself was a primary particle, an ultimate reality.

Respectable universities, before they confer the degree which certifies that the recipient is now wise in philosophy, in science, or in sociology, commonly require a minimum period of "residence." They might well require also a supplementary period of "non-residence," to be passed neither at the university nor in any other populous place but alone. They might consider the fact that a knowledge of one's self is as important as a knowledge of Latin and two modern languages. Already having an athletic field, they might even persuade some wealthy alumnus to make the gift of a Thebaid to which candidates could retire for six months. I can think of nothing more likely to change the direction of our thinking, and many who agree on nothing else agree that it ought to be changed.

Yesterday, before I left the heights, the sun had gone down. There were no clouds in the sky and therefore no Turneresque glory. Instead, there was only a purple glow seeming to come from the air itself, as though the whole lower quarter of the western sky were self-luminous. In its own way the effect was as beautiful as the more flamboyant displays to which clouds contribute and it was also, I am tempted to say, in better taste.

At any rate, it was a sunset and sunsets are still commonly admitted to be Sublime even by those who know them chiefly on postcards or in technicolor. Experimentally, therefore, I addressed myself to it. Wordsworth, I said, found a similar phenomenon adequate proof of the existence of God. What, if anything, do I get out of it? And though I did not get God, I got something. I got proof, if I may put it this way, of the existence of Man—which is doubted rather more often nowadays than the existence of God was doubted in Wordsworth's time.

Few except intellectuals knew then what the rationalism of that age meant. In our day, on the contrary, the very man in the street knows that you must not spell man with a capital letter. He takes it for granted that free will is an illusion; that ideals are the product of class interests; that morality is merely the custom of a group; that consciousness is an epiphenomenon; that what used to be called education is only a process of conditioning the reflexes; and that the "I" itself is only a shifting configuration of impulses, stimuli, and resistances. As for me, I now know better than I ever knew before not only that the man in the twentieth-century street is wrong but what made him so. And I know it because my sky was purple.

Not more than fifty miles from where I stood there is—though I could not see it—a laboratory of physics and in that laboratory are men who would tell me that to call the sky purple is a very loose way of talking. That, they would say, was merely a subjective impression produced in me by the fact that the sky *really was* transmitting to my eye what used to be called ether waves but which probably are something more in the nature of a rhythmic disturbance in a field of electric or gravitational force. And in any event, they would add, the phenomenon of which I was confusedly aware is best described in terms of the number of angstrom units measuring the distance from crest to crest of the disturbance in question.

Now I have not, goodness knows, any disposition to doubt at least part of what they would say. I believe —because I have faith in the methods of science when applied to the problems with which they can deal—that this disturbance in a field of force "really exists" and I find it a source of thrilling amazement to consider that the world of my experience is paralleled by another world of reality so far beyond the reach of my organs of perception. But why should one of these worlds be called realer than the other; why, especially, should the one of which I can have the least experience be called the realest? If the color purple exists only in me, then that proves not only that I exist but proves a good deal more besides. It proves that there is something in the universe which would not be there if I were not. My consciousness, far from being epiphenomenal, is creative. It has created purple. And why, if the color purple "really is," should not all the other things of which I have direct experience be equally real?

One need not, to believe in one universe, deny the other. The reality of the waves and the reality of the color are not mutually exclusive, though they are almost completely discontinuous. No doubt, the grandest reality is the unimaginable synthesis of all the separate ones. But, so far at least, that synthesis is beyond the power of the human mind to make. Every attempt to escape from pluralism ends in the denial that one or the other reality is really real.

There is no reason why an either/or choice should be forced upon us. But if we insist upon making it, why should most men in our day prefer to dismiss as an illusion their most direct experience and give their credence to a supposed ultimate reality which can, at best, be detected so fragmentarily and comprehended so imperfectly that it makes no connection with the reality of everyday life? The chair upon which I sit "really is" an aggregate of vibrating molecules, and perhaps the molecules "really are" only concentrations of energy. But the chair is also the solid object of my experience, and it is with that aspect of its reality that I must live. To live with it successfully, to sit down upon it with confidence, I must believe that it exists. And what goes for the chair goes only not merely for the color purple but also for many other realities of a possibly no less subjective, or man-made, sort.

The physicist who has just demonstrated that the chair as it presents itself to our senses does not really exist presently himself sits down on it. If I should protest that this act makes him guilty of an inconsistency, he would justifiably accuse me of an almost infantile naïveté. And yet, unless he is more philosophical than a great many of his fellow scientists are, he will himself be guilty of a precisely parallel naïveté.

When I think that I am making a decision, he will tell me that I "really am" only hearing a mechanical click as that electronic machine which I call myself calculates correctly the resultant of certain conflicting forces impinging upon it. When I tell him that one thing is "Evil" and that another is "Good," he will tell me that I "really am" only exhibiting the inevitable result of my various conditionings. Nor is even that all. He will insist that though I am perfectly right to live with the chair which can be sat down upon, true wisdom consists in learning to live not with my power of choice or my sense of values, but with what he calls the realities of a mechanist's construction at least as remote from my experience as the undulating purple or the molecular chair.

In the light of such wisdom as his, the educators, the sociologists, the social planners, and the very legislators of our day are attempting to make their "better world" and are not, so far, succeeding so very well. Though one may ask others to live in a universe where a man is nothing in himself but is only a "product of forces," and where Good and Evil are merely the prejudices of a particular culture, no one ever succeeded fully in the attempt to live his own life in that world, ever failed to believe that he himself made decisions, or that he, at least, was right in preferring one thing to another. And it may even be that the psychoanalysts who are looking for the ultimate source of modern man's neurosis could find it right there in the violent conflict between what he tells himself about the human being and what he knows by direct experience to be true of himself.

No mathematician was ever so mad as to suggest that we should try to move bodily into the fourth dimension or even that we should attempt to conduct our practical affairs in accordance with the laws of some non-Euclidian geometry. In our world, parallel lines do not meet and you can't turn an orange wrongside out. Yet "social engineers" want permission to build us a society founded upon premises whose validity—assuming for the sake of argument that they are valid at all—are not consonant with the content of our consciousness and cannot possibly be acted upon as long as consciousness exists. We shall continue to think in terms of Purpose and Will, continue to see both ourselves and others as Good or Evil rather than as merely well- or ill-conditioned almost as long as we continue to see that a sunset is purple.

On my mountaintop, then, two realities met: myself and a color. Whether the second ceased to exist as soon as I turned away is an old, old question answered by philosophical Idealists to their own satisfaction when they insist that, since God is always looking, purple always exists—in His mind if not in the mind of any human being. That answer my readers may take or leave, since the question is not crucial in connection either with what I have said so far or with what I propose to say. As long as I am real and as long as I am looking, the light of that sunset has color just as truly as it has, to the eye of an interferometer, a wave length.

But the end is not yet. As long, at least, as I was there, I could say still another thing about that light in the sky. I could say that it was Beautiful. Here let the materialists throw up their hands if they must. Let them say—as they will—that this is beyond all patience. A sensation may be granted, at a pinch, some sort of shadowy reality, though it is obviously less substantial than a wave length. But Beauty is the mere shadow of a shadow. Though the effect of a sensation may be measured and its occurrence in connection with certain measurable phenomena may be predicted, Beauty is neither measurable nor predictable and for that reason can neither be talked about to any purpose nor reasonably be supposed to exist. Yet the three of us—myself, the color which I saw, and the Beauty of which I was aware—were all there together. If one has already granted the first two, it is too late to deny the third. If the light was not beautiful, the light was not there; and if the light was not there, then neither was I. Perhaps when I departed, God, as the Idealists would say, took over. But whether He did or did not, we three were inseparable as long as I was there. For that period at least the light waves revealed a color and they possessed a value.

Only after I had come down could I spare the time to wonder either how anyone could doubt these facts or, more important, why anyone should want to. Is it only, I wondered, that the novelty of Science and its recent successes have temporarily prejudiced us in its favor? Or can it be that mankind is really moved— as sometimes it seems to be—by some will to self-destruction? Has man deliberately turned away from himself and the universe in which he once flourished? Did he first turn from Nature toward the Machine; then turn from Sight and Hearing toward the Formula and the Instrument; did he, finally, turn away from Will and Value toward Determinism and Ethical Relativity, because he willed his own will-lessness and irresponsibility; because he wanted to destroy ultimately the consciousness in which all the things from which he turned have their being? Does he wish thus, once and for all, to extinguish along with himself everything which, it may be, came into being only with him?

One thing is certain. While the three of us were on the mountaintop I had no impulse to do what the scientist would call "probe deeper" into the realities of which I was aware. I felt no desire to realize that purple "really is" vibrations in the ether or that my awareness of it "really was" a chemical, or perhaps electrical, phenomenon of the brain cells. Whether such probings really are into depths I neither know nor much care; for if it was on the surface that I was, then on the surface is where I, and most human beings, are most truly at home. Beauty, they say, is skin-deep and the saying may be true in a sense rather different from that originally meant. "Last week," wrote Swift, "I saw a woman flayed, and you will hardly believe how much it altered her person for the worse." Yesterday I, on the contrary, saw the bones and flesh of the world clothed in a beautiful skin. I am content to leave to others both the X-ray and the scalpel.

# *Chapter Nine*

# The Individual and the Species

# The Individual and the Species

A few mornings ago I rescued a bat from a swimming pool. The man who owned the pool—but did
not own the bat—asked me why. That question I do
not expect ever to be able to answer, but it involves
a good deal. If even I myself could understand it, I
would know what it is that seems to distinguish man
from the rest of nature, and why, despite all she has to
teach him, there is also something he would like to
teach her if he could.

It is true that I like bats better than most people do.
Though the fact that they fly without feathers is a
heterodoxy held against them since ancient times, I
find it easy to forgive. Moreover, and though I was
exposed at an early age to Gustave Doré's illustrations

for the *Inferno,* I do not associate leathery wings with Satan. I know that their owners have no special predilection for female tresses and "like a bat out of hell" is not, for me, an especially expressive metaphor. But that is not the reason why I took the trouble to rescue one from drowning.

Nature books always explain—for the benefit of utilitarians—that bats are economically important because they destroy many insects. For the benefit of those more interested in the marvelous than in the profitable, they also usually say something about the bat's wonderful invention of a kind of sonar by the aid of which he can fly in the blackest night without colliding with even so artificial an obstruction as a piano wire strung across his path. But before lifting my particular bat out of the swimming pool, I did not calculate his economic importance and I did not rapidly review in my mind the question whether or not his scientific achievement entitled him to life.

Still less could I pretend that he was a rare specimen or that one bat more or less would have any perceptible effect on the balance of nature. There were plenty of others just like him, right here where I live and throughout this whole area. Almost every night I have seen several of his fellows swooping down to the swimming pool for a drink before starting off for an evening of economically useful activity. A few weeks before I had, as a matter of fact, seen near Carlsbad, New Mexico, several hundred thousand of this very species in a single flight. That had seemed like enough bats to satisfy one for a normal lifetime. Yet here I was, not only fishing a single individual from the water, but tending him anxiously to see whether or not he could recover from an ordeal which had obviously been almost too much for him.

Probably he had fallen in because he had miscalculated in the course of the difficult maneuver involved in getting a drink on the wing. Probably, therefore, he had been in the water a good many hours and would not have lasted much longer. But he looked as though he wanted to live and I, inexplicably, also hoped that he would. And that would seem to imply some sort of kindliness more detached, more irrational, and more completely gratuitous than any nature herself is capable of. "So careful of the type she seems, so careless of the single life."

At Carlsbad, so it seemed to me, I had seen bats as nature sees them. Here by the swimming pool, I had seen an individual bat as only man can see him. It was a neat coincidence which arranged the two experiences so close together, and I shall always think of them in that way.

At the cave, I had, of course, plenty of company, since the bats constitute one of the official sights of a National Park. Biologists from distant countries often come specially to see them; but to the ordinary tourist their flight is only a side show, to be taken in after a day underground among the twenty-three miles of explored passages in possibly the most extensive cave in the world. Like Old Faithful in the Yellowstone, the bat eruption is reliably predictable and those unwilling to spend much time on nature can attend a scheduled performance.

About sunset, the very miscellaneous crowd begins to gather, rather nervously uncertain whether it is exhibiting a cultural interest or just being silly. Presently, the park ranger assigned the job of speaking the prologue that evening climbs a boulder to make a little speech, artfully compounded of information and simple, harmless jokes. Tonight, he says, the flight will not be a very large one—probably between two and three hundred thousand bats. Ten years ago, there would have been at least two million, though for once man is not responsible for the declining animal population. The last decade has been unusually dry; that has meant fewer insects and, therefore, fewer bats. Perhaps a relatively wet part of the cycle is about due and the numbers may go up again. But even now there are more than most visitors will care to stay to see.

The bats, he continues, are of the kind called the Mexican free-tailed because the tips of their tails project, as those of most bats do not, a little beyond the leathery membrane which stretches between the hind legs and helps the wings in flight. This bat is the smaller of the two species common in the region, and no one knows how long it has been living in the cave. At least it has been there long enough to lay down vast quantities of guano and hundreds of tons of it were mined out a short generation ago, before chemical fertilizers made the operation unprofitable. Indeed, it was the bats which led to the discovery, within this century, of the caves themselves. Some cowboys went to investigate what they thought was a cloud of smoke from a forest fire, discovered that it was a cloud of bats instead, and thus were led into the caverns which have not yet been explored to their end.

The ranger pauses, and says that it probably won't be long now. The crowd peers down into a black hole which descends very steeply into the ground. Presently someone, like an excited spectator at the race track, shouts "Here they come," as a single bat rises out of the darkness. Less than a quarter of a second later this first-man-out is followed by another, and another, and another until the air is filled by a vast flying squadron. The bats rise, spiraling in a counterclockwise direction up to the rim of the pit, and then disappear as a long stream headed southward. They will all, says the ranger, take a preliminary drink at a stream a mile or so away and then scatter for the night's foraging, to return one by one after a number of hours which depends on how good the hunting is. By morning at the latest, all will have come back to hang, head downward, from the cave wall. And since the young were left behind, each mother must find her way back in the darkness to her particular place among the hundreds of thousands of her fellows.

Every now and then there is a break of a second or two in the steady stream. Then bats begin to erupt again, as though the mouth of the cave were some sort of biological volcano spewing Mexican free-tailed bats in endless number. But no, on second thought, that metaphor will not do, for there is none of the undisciplined confusion of an inanimate explosion. In what order they come I do not know. Perhaps simply in the order of their nearness to the mouth of the cave. Neither, for that matter, do I know how, hanging in darkness, they know that outside the sun has gone down. But in any event, this is not the pell-mell of a mob. In New York, the crowds released from the sky-scrapers do not make their way out of their canyons or into the caves of their subway in any such orderly fashion. There is no pushing, no shoving, no collision. It is like the relentless, disciplined advance of some armada of the air which makes the boasted thousand-plane raids of the latest world war seem puny indeed.

Presently, the spectators begin to drift away in the order of their conscientiousness in "doing" the sights.

Poor as the show is said to be by comparison with the good old days when the Carlsbad bats were really flourishing, it will go on for several hours. Being a medium good sight-seer, I depart at about the time when half of my fellows have already left. As I walk away, I cast my eye back over my shoulder to see that the bats are still coming. For, as Dr. Johnson says, there is a horror in all last things and it may very well be that I shall never see them again.

It is only weeks later that I suddenly remember to ask myself "Why counterclockwise"? Who decided that they should adopt that direction for their spiral, and when did he decide it? Here is a perfect example which Pascal should have known about when he was discussing the fact that it is sometimes less important what a convention is than simply that there should be one. Bat individualists—if, and I doubt it, there are any such things—sensibly confine their protestant be- havior to matters significant in themselves and never undertake to demonstrate that there is more than one way of getting out of this cave.

Or is, perhaps, their apparently sensible behavior really a score for the mechanist? In our part of the world, the water that leaves our bathtubs in a minia- ture whirlpool also spirals counterclockwise because the direction of the earth's rotation tips the otherwise neutral balance in that direction. I have read that in the Southern Hemisphere the normal direction of a vortex is clockwise. Are there bat caves in Africa or in South America and, if there are, then do the bats, I wonder, come out of them clockwise? What would happen if a bat conditioned in the Southern Hemisphere were transported to the north? On all these questions, I had better, I suppose, consult some experts, though I imagine there aren't many. Technically, of course, bats belong to the mammalogists, but because bats are the only mammals which actually fly they don't really fit in anywhere.

Nature abhors a vacuum—in more senses than one. At Carlsbad she found a good place for bats and so she put a great many of them there. In fact, as the recent decline in their numbers neatly illustrates, she filled the place right up to—and no doubt a little beyond—what the food supply could support. If this method of making sure that there will always be as many as possible means that a few of the weaker will always go to the wall that is to her a matter of indifference.

Even I find it difficult to love, in my special human way, as many bats as I saw at Carlsbad. Nature is content to love them in her way and makes no attempt here to love them in the way that even I would fail at. She loves bats in general and as a species. For that reason she can never get enough of them. But as long as there are plenty in the world, she is unconcerned with any particular bat. She gives him his chance (or sometimes his lack of it) and if he does not, or cannot, take it, others will. A margin of failure is to be expected. The greatest good of the greatest number is a ruling principle so absolute that it is not even tempered with regret over those who happen not to be included within the greatest number.

Thus nature discovered, long before the sociologists did, the statistical criterion. Bureaucratic states which accept averages and curves of distribution as realities against which there is no appeal represent a sort of "return to nature" very different from what that phrase is ordinarily taken to imply. Insofar as the great dictators can be assumed to be in any sense sincere when they profess a concern with the welfare of their people or even with that of mankind, their concern is like nature's—indifferent to everything except the statistically measurable result. If they really love men, then they love them only as nature loves bats. She never devised anything so prompt and effective as the gas chamber, but her methods are sometimes almost equally unscrupulous. For she also has her methods— not always pretty ones—of getting rid of what she considers the superfluous. She seems to agree, in principle, with those who maintain that any decisive concern with a mere individual is unscientific, sentimental, and ultimately incompatible with the greatest good of the greatest number.

But one bat in a swimming pool is not the same thing as two or three hundred thousand at Carlsbad. Because there is only one of him and only one of me, some sort of relationship, impossible in the presence of myriads, springs up between us. I no longer take toward him the attitude of nature or the dictator. I become a man again, aware of feelings which are commonly called humane but for which I prefer the stronger word, human.

It was the barking of two young police dogs taking a natural, unsentimental interest in an individual in distress which first called my attention to what I still think of as "my" bat, though I am sure nothing in nature prepared him to believe that I would assume any responsibility for his welfare. At first, I did not know what he was because a fish out of water looks no less inexplicable than a bat in it. The enormous wings attached to his tiny mouse body had helped, no doubt, to keep him afloat, but they were preposterously unmanageable in a dense, resistant medium. The little hooks on his arms by means of which he climbs clumsily on a rough surface were useless on the vertical, tiled sides of the pool. When I lifted him out with a flat wire net, he lay inertly sprawled, his strange body so disorganized as to have lost all functional significance, like a wrecked airplane on a mountainside which does not look as though it had ever been able to take to the air.

A slight shiver which shook his body when I leaned over him was the only sign of life. The situation did not look promising, for I knew that a live bat is very much alive, with a heart which sometimes beats more than seven times as fast as mine. Since he obviously needed—if he was not too far gone to need anything —to be dry and to be warm I spread him on top of a wall in the full sun to which he had never, perhaps, been exposed before. Every now and then the tremor recurred; and as his fur dried, I began to be aware of a heart beating furiously. Possibly, I began to say, he may survive. When I bent closer, he raised his head and hissed in my face, exposing a gleaming set of little white teeth before he collapsed exhausted again.

By now his leathery wings were dry and his fur hardly more than damp. But he still seemed incapable of any except the feeblest movements. I thought that at best it would be hours before he would be able to fly. I put a stone beside him to cast a semishadow and was turning away when I caught sight of something out of the corner of my eye. I looked, just in time to see him raise himself suddenly onto his bony elbows and take off. He half-circled the pool to get his bearings and, flying strongly now, he disappeared from my sight over the desert, not permanently the worse, I hope, for a near escape from the death which would not have been very important so far as the total welfare of the bat community is concerned. Inevitably,

I have wondered whether he has since been among the bats I see drinking at the pool at evening. Or has he, perhaps, found some body of water with less unpleasant associations?

But why had I done more than, like the dogs, peer at him with curiosity? Why had I felt sad when I thought he would never recover, really joyful when I saw him fly away? He is not economically important, however much his tribe may be. If he had drowned, there would have been others left to catch insects as well as to demonstrate for the benefit of science the bat's sonar. Who am I that I should exhibit a concern which, apparently, the Great Mother of bats (and of men) does not share. What did I accomplish for bats, for myself, or for humanity at large when I fished my bat from the water?

These are not rhetorical questions. They probably have several answers, but there is one of which I am especially aware. What I had done was to keep alive an attitude, an emotion, or better yet a strong passion, of which only the faint beginnings are observable in any creature except man and which, moreover, appear in danger of extinction because of two powerful enemies. This sort of concern with a mere individual is scorned alike by the frank apostles of violent unreason and by those proponents of the greatest good for the greatest number who insist upon being what they call scientific rather than what they call sentimental.

Very often I have wondered over the fact that love for humanity seems so often incompatible with love for individual men and women. It seems almost as though most people have to chose one or the other, and it is an often-observed fact, that those who believe themselves great humanitarians are frequently ruthless with acquaintances and dependents alike. They, however, can at least give the specious explanation that concern with the mere individual must not be allowed to confuse the main issue. But what of the less explicable fact that often the kindest and most considerate people seem little concerned with government and politics? Swift boasted his contempt for humanity and his love for John, Tom, and Harry. Anatole France offered the explanation that to love humanity meant to idealize it and therefore to hate most men for not realizing the ideal. But I have sometimes wondered if the paradox were not rooted in something even more fundamental.

It was nature which loved the race, and it was man who added to that a love for the individual as such. Perhaps those two things, though not really incompatible under all circumstances, become so when one accepts also nature's passion for mere numbers. Perhaps, in other words, there really is something incompatible between the value which we put on the individual and nature's insatiable appetite for more and more of every kind of creature, at no matter what cost either to other species or to the individuals of any one species. Perhaps we have retained too much of her immoderate desire for multiplication while developing our own concern for the individual, whom we think of as rare or irreplaceable. Perhaps in other words, it is easiest to love both man and men when there are not too many (or even not too obviously enough) of the last. Perhaps men should not be too common if they are to have value.

One thing is certain. However many of us there may be or come to be, no man and no group of men should have too much power over too many of us. It makes such men or such groups feel too much as though they were nature herself. So careful of the type they are—or claim to be; so careless of the single life they so indubitably become.

# Chapter Ten

# In Search of an Autumn

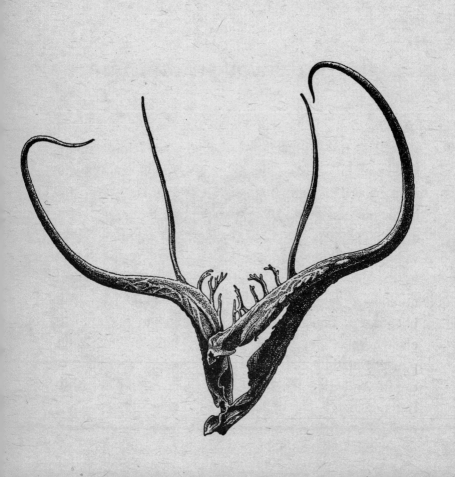

# In Search of an Autumn

I have been told often enough that this climate knows no fall. Spring, they say, sometimes comes even more riotously here than elsewhere, but autumn has no drama. Most of the flowers stop blooming; most of the trees stop growing. The little annual plants wither and blow away; the long bean pods hang brown on the mesquite bushes. But there is no icy blast and no sodden rain to lay the world waste and then put it to sleep. The green earth, never quite so green as elsewhere, is never so brown either. Growing things pause, but they do not surrender even temporarily to death. And what they wait for so quietly is not warmth but moisture.

Very well then, I said, I shall expect no grand effects. Autumn will slip quietly upon us, as the very earliest spring usually does in Connecticut. But where drama is absent nuances are all the more easily appreciated, and nuances there most certainly will be. Southern Arizona is not on the equator. It is not exempt from the consequences of the fact that the axis of the earth is inclined at an angle of twenty-three degrees. This is not Lotus Land, and it is not always afternoon. Many of the human inhabitants probably try, with some success, to forget that seasons exist, but no other animal, I wager, does. Something will tell the rest that some change impends and they will make for it whatever preparation is necessary.

Then, one morning, well before even official, astronomical summer was over, I saw the first unmistakable sign of that preparation where I would not have thought to look. Around scores of the anthills which dot the desert and even the not overly frequented roads, little circles of brown chaff had accumulated until there was perhaps a pint of it in a heap about the main opening of the largest nests. Each pile was composed of the same stuff—the sharp little barbs of a grass which had sprung up after the summer rain and ripened in a few weeks. I bent over to look, and saw that some workers were busy carrying the spikelets into the nest while others, no less busy, were carrying them out again. Could Mark Twain, that great enemy of the ants' reputation for efficiency, be right, and were these little emmets foolishly busy at some sort of boon-doggling invented to satisfy their mania for activity?

But of course the explanation is simple and highly creditable. The one set was gathering the grain; the other, removing the chaff. Somewhere below ground, a threshing bee (or threshing ant) was in progress. No doubt, though I never got around to an investigation, the squirrel's granary, as well as the ant's, would soon be full. And that, on the unimpeachable authority of John Keats, is one of the signs by which autumn may be recognized. His criteria are valid in a latitude for which he never intended them.

Ever since that day when I first realized what the ants were about, I have been on the alert. And now that the end of October has come, I have assured myself by many signs that the autumn, which might have come unnoticed if I had not kept my eyes and ears open, has arrived in its own quiet way. Though the midday temperature still gives no hint of the fact, I fancy that I can notice a diminution in the brilliance of the light now that the sun does not come so close to the zenith as it did in early summer. I think it is that diminished brilliance, rather than any change in the color of the landscape itself, which makes one aware that the color is, indeed, the color of October, not of July.

The thermometer still climbs daily into the middle nineties at noon, and at that moment the sun refuses to admit that it has lost any of its power. The nights, on the other hand, have a different story to tell. Hardly has the sun set than, at this elevation and under skies which seldom have even a light blanket of cloud, the mercury begins to plunge downward. Many a day when it has registered ninety-five at 1:00 P.M. it stands at fifty-five just before dawn. Forty degrees is a tremendous drop, something which New England knows only at the onset of a phenomenal cold wave. Here it is almost a daily occurrence, and not everyone finds it agreeable. Quite a few, when they get up in the morning, are reminded by twinges of lumbago and sciatica that they are equipped with backs. I, who love warmth, pull the covers around me and slip back into sleep, dreaming happily of the fact that before many hours have passed I shall be strolling coatless, perhaps even shirtless, in the sun.

Here as elsewhere, many of the birds migrate. Some pass only the summer or only the winter in this region; others, with a taste for more violent contrasts, pass through on their way from much farther north to much farther south. Ornithologists think now that they have a better explanation of the phenomenon than they used to have, but their conviction that the northern movement in summer is for the sake of the longer feeding day would be a little more convincing if it were not for the fact that what is north for one species is south for another. An irresponsible person like myself is tempted to wonder if it may not be simply that the birds, too, like a change. In my own East, South Carolina is a winter resort for some New Yorkers though others, like the South Carolinians themselves, go all the way to Florida. And in exactly the same way, some northern birds come to Arizona for the winter, while some Arizona birds who have been here all summer go to Mexico or Central America for their winter vacation.

In any event, it all contributes to variety, for the observer as well as for the birds. A few weeks ago I saw on a bush just outside my door the beautiful pileolated warbler—as yellow as the yellow warbler of the east but with a jet-black cap on his head. My book tells me that it summers no farther south than the northern parts of the state and that it merely passes through here on its way to some farther destination not specified. Other birds, said to include this region in their summer range, have become much more numerous now that the residents have been joined by individuals who passed the summer elsewhere. The desert sparrow, for example—one of the prettiest of all his tribe—I saw only rarely until a few weeks ago, when flocks began to frequent the patio. On the other hand, the white-winged dove ceased his cock-a-doodle-doing long ago and I see him no more. Gambel's quail still wander about like barnyard fowl; I cannot help thinking that they must be almost as surprised as such barnyard fowl would be when the open season arrives and hunters, to whom they must furnish as much "sport" as would the Public Library pigeons in New York, begin to bang away at them. The road-runner stays too, and so do some of the most abundant and vociferous of all: the gilded flicker and the Gila wood-pecker, who scream from the saguaros; the chatter-ing cactus wren, twice as big as a wren should be; and Palmer's thrasher, whose impudent, two-syllable whistle reminds one irresistibly of a truck driver who has just seen a blonde. Though I am no ornithologist and don't know where to look for birds, I have already counted more than fifty species either from the door-yard or in the course of casual walks.

Before the end of December, so they tell me, we will certainly have frost, probably even ice, during the nightly plunge of the thermometer. For that rea-son, oranges will grow here only in specially favored spots and only if carefully protected. During the night, I can believe that frost will come; at midday, I lapse into incredulity, and they say it is the same even in mid-winter, when it is hard to remember at noon that it was cold a few hours before.

Perhaps those frosts will bring visible changes in the landscape greater than any I have been able to detect so far, but I still have to take account of little details when I try to justify my determination to be

aware of a season. A few purple asters bloom by the
roadside, but one must look for them with an eye
trained in New England to regard them as a sign that
summer is almost over. Many other weeds along the
highways are still blooming profusely in late October,
and it is rather by the presence of fruits than by the
absence of flowers that one recognizes autumn. The
round, yellow gourds which one did not see when
they were green are hanging from the vines, draped
over a shrub if they could find one, trailing along the
ground if they could not. Desert cats and dogs now
stop every few minutes to remove from their feet the
hard, spiny little fruits of a prostrate weed which the
learned call *Tribulus terrestris,* the vulgar call "punc-
ture vine," and the historically minded know got its
family name, Caltrops, from those wicked iron burrs
which medieval strategists used to scatter over the
ground across which an enemy cavalry was expected
to attack.

Human walkers sometimes find a caltrops inside
their shoes, but they are more likely to find clinging
to their clothing the most extraordinary of all desert
fruits—a pair of four- or five-inch horns, curved like
the horns of a longhorn steer but further embellished
with a second pair of smaller hooks placed between
the two main horns at exactly that different angle
which will produce the most pleasing aesthetic effect.
All in all, it is so accomplished a piece of modern de-

sign that I have asked Mr. Freund to use a repre-
sentation of it on the title page of this book.

To my amazement, I discovered that it is the fruit
of that rather coarse prostrate annual whose gaudy
yellow and purple blossoms were among the first
things I noticed when the flowers came out after the
earliest midsummer rains. Martynia is the botanical
name, devil's horn one of the popular ones; but
the finished product—which looks so much as though
Georgia O'Keeffe had imagined it—is so totally different from the rather homely green fruit that I could
not imagine how an oversized okra pod with a curved
beak at one end could be transformed into so extraordinary a work of art, carrying with it, as it does, the
somewhat sinister suggestions of a modern style. I
picked several and watched them dry in the sun, only
to discover that the process is one of elegant simplicity.
The pod begins to split at the pointed end; the two
halves separate, as they curve back, to form the major
horns; the two delicate supplementary horns split off
neatly to assume their own different line of curvature;
finally, the skin peels off the whole, leaving a perfectly
proportioned "object in space." No technique for
achieving significant form could be more expert or
more economical.

If there is anything in the chamber of commerce
claims that we live longer out here than we do in the

East, then perhaps it is less because of anything merely physical than because of a certain psychological salubriousness in the climate. Seasons, entertaining though they are, do nevertheless remind us that time is passing. When one summer comes to an end, we remember that the total number of our summers is not limitless. Every New England autumn is a kind of *memento mori* which grows more threatening at every recurrence. And perhaps where it is so easy not to notice the phases of a cycle we do not realize how long we are living. Perhaps there are some who simply forget to die.

In any event—and chambers of commerce aside—there is an indisputable appropriateness in a mild autumn to introduce a mild winter. In New England, the blaze of color and the sudden descent of leaves which cover the earth is a fitting prelude to what is to follow—temporary death for most living things and the coming domination of snow and ice. Here, the minor phenomena announce only what is more a mere shift of emphasis than it is a revolution.

Those who feel that they simply must have something more dramatic than what I have described will have to climb for it. As a matter of fact, it might be said that the seasons here are more a matter of vertical distance than of time, for with mountains of imposing height scattered casually about through most parts of Arizona and New Mexico one is never at any season of the year very far from a totally different climatic zone. Three-quarters of an hour in an automobile and less than thirty miles in horizontal distance takes one from the Lower Sonoran Desert, where it is summer even in October, to an altitude of seven thousand feet, where it is, by now, autumn even according to a New Englander's standards. As one mounts, the saguaro and paloverde disappear quite suddenly to give way to evergreens and, in the moister situations, to cottonwood and sycamore also. Even several weeks ago the cottonwoods up there were already as unmistakably autumnal as anything in New England, and all the trees were full of birds, many of whom never descend to a lower region.

This is one of the reasons why, as Roger Tory Peterson tells his readers, there are more nesting land birds in southeastern Arizona than in any other area of comparable size in the United States. "There are places in the Southwest where we can go through five or six life zones in half a day. . . . To accomplish such a change of scene in the East, we should have to journey two thousand miles, from Florida to the Gaspé or Newfoundland." It is also why the flora is as varied as the bird population, and why, if one includes the region of the San Francisco Peaks near the middle of the state, one can say that the plant life covers every climatic division from the subtropical to the alpine.

In fact, some of the very same plants growing on the mountaintops grow also within the Arctic Circle.

Interesting as these facts are—and I have verified some of them for myself—I have a feeling that to climb for one's autumn is plain cheating. What counts is what is here. I will not consider the mountaintops, no matter how accessible, for the same reason that I would not consider the effects of a journey I might make by jet plane to the Dakotas in not much more time.

But to *look* up is certainly legitimate. The sky above is as much a part of a given place as the earth beneath, and the stars know, if the plants and animals do not seem to, that the earth has moved. This year it so happens that, as dusk falls, Jupiter, riding high in the sky, is suddenly there while twilight is still bright almost to brilliance; and his presence reminds one to watch for the appearance, one by one, of the stars which are no longer where they were at twilight a few months ago.

The fields of heaven have changed more than those of earth. Despite the disappearance of many summer blossoms, the world is still almost as green, with the subdued greenness of the desert, as it ever was. But overhead one will find, if one has not recently looked, an unfamiliar spectacle. Scorpio, so conspicuous a few months ago, now sets soon after dusk, with Sagittarius following in his eternal, hopeless pursuit. The Big Dipper now dips so soon behind the mountains which close my northern horizon that one would have to get to bed very early indeed not to outwatch the Bear. But the Pleiades are much sooner up, and before long Aldebaran, true to his Arabic name, follows them out of the east. Orion, who did not rise in August until early morning, now puts in his appearance before midnight with his belt and his sword between the blaze of Betelgeuse and the blaze of Rigel. For a long time to come they will join me earlier and earlier and soon even the Dog Star, brightest of all, will be visible. Once already, when I was up before dawn, I saw him burning so fiercely that I can well understand why the ancients supposed that when, in summer, he rode invisible across the sky close beside the sun, his presence was responsible for the unusual heat of the dog days.

Nothing else in the visible world can be counted on so surely as these scheduled spectacles of the sky. Nowhere does January bring snow or April bring showers with anything like such ineluctable certainty. The stars' unvarying cycle of changes is the most nearly dependable phenomenon which has come under human observation. Every night they move across the heavens in fixed relation to one another, as though they were indeed borne 'round and 'round on the inner surface of a great, eternally revolving sphere. If we could see them for twenty-four hours a day, the monotony of their march might well, by now, have modified profoundly man's feeling about the universe in which he lives. Even as it is, every season of every year sees them return at a given hour to the exact point they occupied the year before. This, we are inclined to say, is the one thing which can be counted upon, the one thing which certainly always was and always will be just so and no otherwise.

Yet this apparent changelessness is only apparent. The "fixed" stars are only relatively fixed—relative, that is, to the brief span of our own lives. "As changeless as the stars in their courses" is not really changeless and thus, though nothing else in all our experience seems so immobile as the polestar, even it also moves.

Between the time when it was first pointed out to our childish eyes and the time when, on our dying day perhaps, we will look up at it for the last time, it will not have seemed to move, no matter at what hour or what season we may look. Yet in twelve thousand years, so they tell me, it will have moved so much that Vega, which now blazes near the zenith on an autumn evening and then declines toward the west, will be where Polaris now is and will rest there, apparently immobile, while all the other stars, including Polaris itself, make their circles about it. In another twelve or thirteen thousand after that, Polaris and Vega will be back again where they now are.

This "precessionary" cycle of the equinoxes is complete in a little more than twenty-five thousand years and that is the longest cycle of recurring events about which we know anything. Yet it has fulfilled itself many times since the earth's history began and may fulfill itself many more before it ends.

Beyond the limits of that cycle, even the most learned astronomers can only guess at the meaning of a perceptible drift in the whole solar system. Is that drift part of some vaster circling which it will take even longer to complete and are we swinging through some orbit too vast to compute, or are we *really* drifting away from some point in space to which we shall never return, toward some unimaginable destination? That question is beyond even speculation. Perhaps we are following the curve of space and perhaps, after an infinity of time, we will come back again to where we now are, back from a journey which took us an infinite distance. The one thing we do know is that the most fixed of known points is not really fixed at all.

"Whither the Movies?", "Whither Democracy?", "Whither Mankind?". A thousand editorials have asked these questions. "Whither?" indeed. Meanwhile, in the Lower Sonoran Desert, the ant's granary is full and so too, presumably, is the squirrel's.

# Chapter Eleven

# Tour of Inspection

# Tour of Inspection

During more than eight months I stuck close to my own little stretch of cactus and sand. I never wandered more than a few hours away from my house, never passed a night under any other roof. Every morning I looked out of the same window to see the birds assembled at the same feeding ground; every evening watched the shadows begin to fill the valleys in the same mountain range. By now this was home in the simplest sense of that word. It was, I mean, the place where one opens one's eyes without surprise. Home can mean a great deal more, but it can hardly mean less. This is a minimal definition, and the place where I was fulfilled it.

Perhaps, I said to myself, I can now risk a brief

journey. Though every noon is still balmy and though nature will not know a real winter sleep, she has, nevertheless, fallen into a sort of doze and I will not be likely to miss anything important. The lizards, to whom even the first cool nights must have seemed boreal, disappeared long ago, and by now I can hardly believe I ever saw or heard those strange toads who made, in July, their brief appearance. Though the birds still sing occasionally, their enthusiasm is drastically reduced; and if an occasional flower breaks out on an herb or tree it is with the air of making an absent-minded mistake. Spring, they say, does not begin until about the last week in February, and for at least another six or seven weeks nothing much will happen. Moreover, I said, a week will certainly not be long enough to uproot me. I will still feel that there is one place I belong to. When I come back, it will be with a sense of return. And so I set out to be, for a few days, not a resident but a mere sight-seer again.

Fortunately, the very night before I left, something happened to remedy the one deficiency I had so far felt in my eight months' experience: I had seen no strange stars and I was almost resigned to the fact. The heavens had refused to recognize my change of scene, refused to gratify my pride of displacement. "So far as I am concerned," said the sky, "you have not gone anywhere, you have hardly even moved perceptibly." And then—thinking of quite other things—I suddenly caught sight of a brilliant point of twinkling light just above the southern horizon, where no conspicuous star should be. I rubbed my eyes. An airplane? A light in some distant window always dark before? Then, after a moment's bewilderment, came the realization of what had actually happened. It could only be Canopus, brightest star of the Southern Hemisphere and, next to Sirius, the brightest of the whole firmament.

In midwinter he rises just above this horizon, and he was winking at me coyly before dropping promptly out of sight again. "Even by our standards," he was saying, "you have come just this perceptible distance. Even in the heavens you can see something you would never have seen in New England. That inverted bowl you call the sky is not a bowl at all. It is not a hemi-anything. It is a sphere. Move south three times as far again as you came last spring and the whole of it will be exposed to you at one hour or another since at the equator no star fails sometimes to rise and none ever fails to set. There and there only could you see the whole show. But at least you have now added one star."

The reason, or at least the excuse, for my winter jaunt was the desire to refresh my memory of some deserts other than "mine" and to assure myself again that I had made the best choice when I selected this particular one. "Desert" is, of course, a term almost as general as "wood" or "mountain," and even within the

American Southwest there is wide variety. West of my own Lower Sonoran, the geographers recognize two—the Mojave and the Colorado—which are geographically distinct both from the Sonoran and from one another. Ecologists, thinking in terms of plant and animal life, describe them with words drawn from their special vocabulary. Even the mere tourist recognizes great differences, though he ordinarily does not realize very precisely what those differences are. My jaunt took me across the Colorado Desert to San Diego and then, by a slightly more northern route, back across part of the Mojave. It was a great deal to try to take in during seven short days, but I had at least seen it all several times before and I was prepared, as I never had been, to understand the significance of what I saw.

"Home" is in the middle of the Lower Sonoran, on a dry plateau about twenty-five hundred feet above sea level and almost encircled by mountains. To go northwest and then due west for about two hundred and fifty miles is to slip between the surrounding heights, to drop steadily yet almost imperceptibly down, and to reach at Yuma on the Arizona–California border a region which is a mere hundred and fifty feet above sea level. To press on westward for another one hundred and fifty miles is soon to find oneself threading mountain passes above which rise five-thousand-foot peaks and then, just before the coast is reached, to slide precipitously down to the subtropical beaches of Southern California.

Turning north then for a few miles before striking eastward on the return journey, we climb up the coastal range, all but drop off its summit down the eastern side, and then, in an hour or two, find ourselves, at the edge of the Salton Sea, a little Salt Lake nearly two hundred and fifty feet below sea level and thus only a dozen feet above the lowest point on the North American Continent. Between the Salton Sea and "home" there then lies, first a goodly stretch of the Mojave and, across the Colorado River, our own Lower Sonoran again.

In that whole circular journey of about a thousand miles, there is, except for a few man-made oases, very little country that is not desert of one kind or another. West of Yuma one crosses for a few miles the lower end of the Imperial Valley whose hot, irrigated lowlands magically conjure up annually thousands of tons of lettuce and cantaloupes which flow eastward to every city and town on the Atlantic seaboard. On the return journey one may turn a few miles off the main road into what looks like a more and more arid waste until one comes suddenly upon the improbable little settlement called Borego, where a few fields, green as Vermont, lie in the middle of the scorching plain which stretches away as far as the eye can reach. In an automobile, these little verdant anomalies are soon forgotten, almost discredited, as soon as they are passed, and one gets used to expecting no sort of variety except that possible to the different kinds of dryness.

Yet the variety which can be achieved within the limitations imposed by the one invariable condition—scarcity of water—is astonishing. If nature were nowhere wetter, one might still spend a lifetime marveling at her copious inventiveness. Mountain differs from plain, but so too does mountain from mountain or plain from plain. Wherever there is a difference of altitude, or rainfall, or soil texture, there is a corresponding difference in the character as well as the extent of the vegetation, which never actually clothes the earth but is almost everywhere more or less abundantly sprinkled over it.

Some volcanic mountains, mere piles of boulders, seem almost bare until one looks carefully enough to become aware of the fact that thorny shrubs have found crevices to spring from, and that here and there a "century plant" has lived long enough to send up one of those strange, treelike stalks of blossoms which may not require a century of preparation but which do make their appearance only after the plant has spent ten years or more gathering strength to send them aloft just before it dies. Near Yuma, the low-lying sand dunes, hot as few other regions in the United States are hot, get so little rain, even by desert standards, that that vegetation is almost as nearly nonexistent as on the Sahara, and by comparison, my own desert looks almost lush. But between these extremes—if from dry to drier can be called an extreme—lies every possible degree of difference.

Sometimes the line between one region and another is drawn almost as sharply as the timber line on a mountainside, and one can step from one to the other, saying "Here the land of cactus and paloverde ends; here that of creosote bush and small annual herbs begins." Thus the Colorado River marks almost absolutely the western boundary of the giant saguaro. And though two of the desert's other strange inventions, the Joshua tree and the smoke tree, do invade the western edge of Arizona, they belong essentially to the Mojave, not to the Lower Sonoran.

The Joshua tree, grotesque rather than beautiful, with its bare trunk and its spreading branches, also bare except for the clump of yucca leaves which seem to have got mysteriously attached to their extremities, attracts the attention of the most casual traveler. The smoke tree, though more beautiful, blends so perfectly into its surroundings that one must look for it if one is to be more than vaguely aware of the tangled masses of twigs, gray green and usually leafless, which lie here and there like little puffs of cloud on the sand. Except during the time of blossom, the desert employs pastel shades exclusively, and none is more delicate than that of the smoke tree.

We xerophylophiles (and I offer the word to the dictionary makers who have sometimes accepted worse) do not always agree with one another over the question just where the particular style of beauty which we admire reaches its perfection. Some Californians speak as though the Mojave—whose defect, if it has one, is a kind of monotony—were the only desert deserving the name. Others cannot get along without sagebrush, which is not really characteristic of any region so far south as this. There are even those who prefer the dry grasslands which cover certain of the upland regions along the eastern portions of the Arizona–Mexican border, but which the rest of us dismiss as pleasant enough in their own way though hardly to be called desert in any sense of the word. As for me, I returned from my tour of inspection confirmed in the opinion that I had chosen well, and that, without invidiousness, I could say, "Nothing else quite equals, for day by day contemplation, my own Lower Sonoran Desert."

I like even its relatively uninteresting flats, where the fine, hard-packed, and rather sandy soil supports little except the unconquerable creosote bush, crowding into thickets if conditions are relatively favorable and growing at thirty-foot intervals where conditions are a little hard even for a creosote bush. I like better the upper slopes of the higher mountains, where the evergreens have not yet begun and the ocotillo and the agave are most at home. But I like best of all those in-betweens which ecologists call the upper bajadas and in the middle of one of which I have been living.

These are the great stretches of country which form a border, miles wide, around the bases of the foothills. Typically, they lie at less than three thousand feet above sea level and the topsoil—if you can call it that —is composed exclusively of the detritus of the weathered mountains. It is stony and loose enough so that when rain does fall the water neither runs off in an instant, as it does from the steep slopes, nor merely lies on the surface for an hour or two until evaporated from the compact surface of the flats. Instead, it sinks a few inches into the rubble and remains there long enough for the plants to take it up into the tissues prepared for storing. The saguaro, the cholla cactus, and the prickly pear find it ideal, and so does the paloverde. All of them flourish so abundantly that they are as characteristic there as the creosote is on the flatlands or the evergreens on the real mountaintops. They give its character to what is the "succulent desert" par excellence, and from the standpoint of vegetation at least there is no other kind of desert so startlingly *sui generis*.

Nevertheless, and as even I will admit, there is much to be said on all sides. I came back more than ever convinced not only that all these southwestern deserts are exhilarating, but also that, considered not botanically, or geographically, or zoologically, but spiritually they are more alike than different. They please the eye and pique the curiosity in different ways, but what they do to the soul is much the same everywhere. And that is, in the end, the most important thing.

Moreover, now that I am back, I think that I understand better than I did before what it is that they do to the soul, why I find this country more than merely aesthetically satisfying, and why its spaciousness as well as its austerity are more than merely physically—and nervously—reassuring to those who have found the great centers too crowded and too tense. Call it, if you must, only another aspect of the pathetic fallacy, but the desert seems to approve and to encourage an attitude with which I have found scant sympathy among men, and of which I have never before been quite so sure that even nature approved. However fanciful this may seem or, for all I care, however fanciful it may actually be, all the deserts seem to suggest and confirm a system of values for which much ought to be, but very seldom is, said.

In contemporary society, the all but universal ambition of the individual and the all but invariable aim of every proposed social or political movement is to get, for oneself or for others, more *things*. Even those who insist that if the aim is happiness or contentment the desire for material wealth is a fallacy, are nevertheless sure that to be richer in material things is what society as a whole needs to make mankind happier and more contented. The Liberal, so-called, and the Reactionary, so-called, accuse one another of unreason and of selfishness. But the dispute is only over who shall get what proportion of the More, never over the question whether or not more of the kind of thing being disputed over is what is really needed.

In the atmosphere which the dispute generates, in the world where the disputants live, it becomes more and more difficult for the skeptic to understand his own half-formulated protest that there are things not material of which one might have more; that even material things, good in themselves, are sometimes purchased at too high a price if that price is the acceptance of less and less of certain other things; and that the index which determines a "standard of living" ought to take account of factors not usually included.

In the desert, on the other hand, the very fauna and flora proclaim that one can have a great deal of certain things while having very little of others; that one kind of scarcity is compatible with, perhaps even a necessary condition of, another kind of plenty—for instance, on even the level of things tangible or visible, that plenty of light and plenty of space may go with a scarcity of water.

By analogy, that reminds one that "economy of abundance" is a meaningless phrase unless one asks, "Abundance of what?". A society could have an abundance of physical space and also an abundance of spiritual space. It could have an abundance of leisure, of contemplation, of intellectuality, and of spirituality. It might even have an abundance of manners. And it might have all these things without having any more of many other things; might indeed find it easier to keep the one abundance if it did not have thrust upon it more of the other.

Yet of this obvious fact few seem ever to think. Most take it for granted that the abundance which is desirable is the abundance which manifests itself most conspicuously in, say, juke boxes, television sets, organized playgrounds, and even, perhaps, of schools and of museums. They seem not even aware of the fact that much has grown scarcer while these things have been becoming more abundant, and that many things threaten to grow even scarcer still.

I am no ascetic and, so at least I believe, no fanatic of any other sort. I am not praising want and I have no romantic notion that distresses should not be relieved. But I do, in all seriousness, question the assumption that endless progress implies the endless multiplication of goods and gadgets, even that "real wages" and "production per man hour" are necessarily an approximate index of welfare. I am not saying that a reduction in the standard of material living automatically brings with it an increase in happiness or nobility, but I do doubt that the converse is true, and I do find it astonishing that this doubt seems so seldom shared.

If what I find in the desert is no example to be imitated, it suggests a metaphor which to me is meaningful. What I learn by way of this metaphor is not the kind of thing I learn from a treatise on economics or even on morals. But it is very much the kind of thing I learn from an essay by Emerson or a poem by Emily Dickinson. And a world which seems to have passed long ago the point where treatises on economics or on morals begin to pay a sadly diminished return in wisdom might do well to pay more attention to what poets—and deserts—have striven to communicate in their own way.

When I go back, as I must, to live in a world almost wholly man-made and almost wholly absorbed in problems which man himself has created, I shall often return in memory to things seen and done during my desert interlude. There will be, first of all, encounters with birds and beasts to be remembered. Then, as on a screen, I shall see my mental kodachromes projected—sometimes of vast vistas of mountain or plain, sometimes little close-ups of an improbable blossom bursting out of a cactus, or of a lizard poised for a moment in the sun. All too often, I am afraid, I shall be reminded how whole acres of New York City in which nothing grows have been turned into a desert far more absolute than any I have ever seen in the Southwest, and I shall wonder whether man himself can live well in a place where nothing else can live at all. But I doubt whether anything else will be so continuously in the back of my mind as the consciousness of that metaphor which two thousand miles of countryside set forth, and I shall not forget its lesson: much can be lacking in the midst of plenty; on the other hand, where some things are scarce others, no less desirable, may abound.

# Chapter Twelve

# The Metaphor
## of the Grasslands

# The Metaphor
## of the Grasslands

I suppose that most of even the desert is owned or
leased. Despite appearances, a good deal of it is economically valuable and in certain semidesert areas
ranchers grow rich off the cattle one rarely sees. In
such sections, as well as in even less promising looking areas, wire fences surprise one into the realization
that what looks like mere abstract space is actually
private property. Outside the national forests and Indian reservations there is little land which does not
belong to someone.

Despite this legal fact, a great deal of it seems very
loosely held in any sense except the legal. "Keep Out"
signs are rare, the wanderer seldom has any sense of
trespassing, and for his purposes, the country belongs

to him as much as to anyone else. He could not raise cattle or dig mines on it, but he may exploit its spiritual resources as freely as he is able. He will not come upon anything like that little, foot-wide triangle of mosaic set into a sidewalk in New York which reads: "This area is the property of the Blank estate and has never been dedicated to public purposes." *De minimis non curat lex*, but half a square foot of metropolitan real estate is not a small thing.

The sense that out here even ownership cannot enforce very jealously its rights is no doubt another of the reasons why one feels a certain relaxation of the pressures which bear in upon us from every direction in more fully "developed" regions. In them even the nonhuman co-dwellers are unwelcome and are reduced to the status of vermin to be exterminated as far as possible until the very sparrows and pigeons are regarded as mere nuisances, and the city dweller has as his ideal the complete sterilization of the area he occupies. Here the owner must share his ownership with the jack rabbit, the gopher, and the road-runner whether he likes it or not. He is unlikely to see even the human trespasser, and unlikely to bristle if he does.

Thoreau boasted that he had got more good out of many a New England plot than the farmer in whose name the deed was registered and that, in this sense, he was most truly the one who owned it. But it required on Thoreau's part a good deal of imagination to feel this way, and what was, for him, an ingenious paradox comes very close to being a simple fact in these more spacious regions. Certainly I never expect to own in any legal sense the one-thousandth part of so much land as I have exploited during the past months and from which I could not have got more if I had bought it all from the nominal owners. They paid the taxes and rode range on the cattle, while I got the real good of it all. And what is more, I cannot be sued.

It is not, I hasten to add, that my ideal approaches any sort of communism near enough to make me wish that nothing could ever be owned more exclusively or more effectively than thousands of acres of Arizona desert are owned. Out of certain other things—as well as out of smaller sections of the land itself—the spiritual as well as the material good can be enjoyed only when they are exclusively and jealously held. There are things which can and should be owned, as there are things which cannot; things which indiscriminate sharing destroys, as well as things which can be enjoyed only if they are open freely to others. But large sections of space are not among the things which ought to be owned; and where there are so many people that, if each is to possess jealously the little he needs, then there is nothing left over for general ownership, the situation is disastrous, physically as well as spiritually. In such regions it is almost as though the sky itself were parceled out and no man could enjoy another man's star. A star or a constellation is, indeed, the perfect example of the sort of thing which does not need to be owned. Its relation to you is not modified by its relation to anyone else. You cannot do anything for it or anything to it. No matter how many men are looking at Arcturus, each is alone with it because contemplation is always solitary.

But there are other examples equally good of things which mean most when, sometimes nothing until, one can say with all the pride of possession "This is mine." The "nationalization of women" was sometimes dismissed as no more than a bugaboo invented by the bourgeoisie, but it comes close to the heart of the matter—as Milton knew when he admitted that Adam and Eve belonged to one another and that this mutual ownership represented the "sole propriety in Paradise of all things common else." Whatever a man can do something to and for comes within the category of those things which may, under certain circumstances, be properly owned. There are some things which belong to no one if they belong to everybody, and some kinds of love must not be spread too thin. Just as no one can care for a child—cynics would say "put up with a child"—

like those to whom he belongs, so can no one do for a house what its owner can. What we alone are responsible for we are responsible for in a unique way. We do something to it and it does something to us; and for the emotions which accompany that kind of ownership there is no substitute.

Conceivably, the time might come when warmth of this sort no longer existed in the world because the situations which generate it could no longer arise in the kind of society which had been permitted to develop. Conceivably, men might live in houses temporarily assigned them by the state and maintained at a certain standard level of comfort and efficiency. Conceivably, they might enjoy only, and at stated hours, the flowers and the birds maintained for them in the People's Park for Culture and Recreation. Conceivably, even, they might never imagine any relationship with a child except as an anonymous inmate of a state nursery, and no relationship with a member of the opposite sex except such as was required of them during periodic visits to the breeding stable. But such a society would not be simply one in which the emotions we know had been re-channeled. They would have ceased to exist, and there would be something which is, to us, almost supremely important for which no equivalent was even suspected. What goes along with certain kinds of ownership is absolutely *sui generis*.

A few days ago I drove deep into a canyon which shelters some of the remotest of the ranching country. I took my car over the bumps rather more carefully than I would probably have done had it belonged to the State or "the people" rather than to me, but it was not with the moral of this fact that I was most concerned. Here, it seemed to me, was one isolated example of certain kinds and degrees of ownership happily combined.

In the most intimate sense of the word, these ranchers owned the ranch house and its immediate surroundings. They had planted the cottonwoods, and they cherished the dogs and the cats. A certain enclosure was private, and they would have resented my too free intrusion upon it. In addition, they owned legally I know not how many thousands of acres. But they held all these outlying slopes and meadows and cliffs far more loosely in a spiritual, as well as in a practical, way. For one thing, they did, and could do, much less to these areas. Whatever large general measures of "range control" they may have practiced, wild nature was pretty much having her way. Various birds and beasts, each in his own fashion, "owned" their territories, unaware of any overlapping of human or animal proprietorship; the mesquite, the saguaro and the barrel cactus grew where they found it agreeable to grow. Here man was able to live in nature without being compelled, as in cities he is compelled, to destroy her. There was no attempt to assert control, to be jealously possessive, beyond the limits within which possessiveness is justified by its fruits. If anyone saw me intruding upon his property, it is not likely that he resented the intrusion. The land was his but it was also, so far as I was concerned, almost as much a "People's Park" as though it had been called something like that.

I am attributing no special virtue to the rancher and I am not suggesting that all society might be organized as his is. Perhaps both he and his place in nature are the product of those "conditions" which in some schools of sociology assume the role of a final cause. I am saying only that thanks to chance or to what-you-will one finds here a happy example of how the characteristic goods of proprietorship may co-exist with those of a kind of communism; saying also that just as there is a metaphor of the desert, so too there is a metaphor of the grasslands; that this ranch country also may be enjoyed as a kind of poem.

What this poem says when properly interpreted is something like this: One can own, either rightfully or fruitfully, only those things—and only so much of a thing—as one can come into some intimate relationship with. One cannot really own any land to which one does not in turn belong, and what is true of land is true of everything else. One can own only what one loves, and love is always some sort of reciprocal relationship. I may buy a thing when I have the money to pay for it, but I do not actually possess it until I have allowed it, in some sense, to possess me.

It is this, of course, which explains the tragedy or the comedy of that class of rich men who accumulate so much and possess so little. Their houses are full of books they never read, pictures they never see, and pianos they never play. They buy more and more because they are always hoping, in vain, that they will achieve at last the sense that something belongs to them. They take title to estates and farms and ranches. At their command, barns are stocked, gardens appear, and flowers bloom. But that much cannot belong to anyone because no one can belong to that much. The owners gaze helplessly at what is said to be theirs, but they have no inner conviction that it is. At most, they can get no more out of their estates than the humble citizen gets out of a public park into which he has wandered on an off day. By trying to have too much, these rich accumulators have made it impossible to have anything.

I have never believed that "property is theft" or even that a thing necessarily belongs to him who needs it most or can use it best. At least, I do not see how men could live well together on the basis of any such assumption. But the proposition does have an obverse. This obverse states a principle which, like all laws of nature, operates everywhere and always, without waiting for a society to incorporate it into the kind of law which courts must enforce. If things do not necessarily belong to those who need and can use them, it is nevertheless certainly true that nothing can really belong to anyone *unless* he needs and can use it. "Under the present system" men may take title to much they cannot own. Sometimes they may thus dispossess those who could. But, at most, they exclude others from something they cannot themselves have.

From a poem by Emerson I learned long ago the grimmest section of this law, the final be-it-enacted, which provides that no matter how much one loves and therefore truly possesses, the time must come when one can no longer love and therefore no longer possess anything:

> "Here is the land,
>   Shaggy with wood,
>   With its old valley,
>   Mound and flood. . . ."
> "They called me theirs,
>   Who so controlled me;
>   Yet every one
>   Wished to stay, and is gone,
>   How am I theirs,
>   If they cannot hold me,
>   But I hold them?"

The poem I have more recently read in the grasslands seems to prefer to emphasize the more cheerful aspects of the general law. It explains and celebrates a kind of ownership which is real, at least while it lasts, as well as innocent and fruitful. It even goes a little beyond that, revealing to me how, if I have much love though little money, I may enjoy and therefore possess much that "belongs" to someone else.

# Chapter Thirteen

## Spring

# Spring

Half a dozen friends have written me from the East to ask if I heard the peepers this year. I didn't, of course—either literally or figuratively. Not literally, because *Hyla crucifer* does not cross the Great Plains; not figuratively, because where there is no real winter there cannot be anything to announce that it is over.

Today, the fifteenth of May, is, I suppose, a part of summer. At least the temperature has been more than once above ninety and many plants have already gone to seed. But I should be hard put to it to say when either spring or summer began. Where there is no month in which flowers do not bloom, one can only consult the almanac or the sky if one insists upon establishing a fixed point.

Even among the growing things themselves there seems to be no general agreement. The deciduous trees, seemingly determined to continue the customs appropriate to the climate of regions where their tribe is dominant, go through the form of a winter rest, though even they cannot agree among themselves as to its proper duration. Along the washes, cottonwoods began to glow greenly sometime after the middle of March, while the mesquites of the desert remained dry and dead for another five or six weeks, until, in response to no obvious stimulus, they suddenly burst into leaf and blossom. Meanwhile, both had been preceded by many other phenomena as indisputably vernal.

Little suspecting the bewilderment I was preparing for myself, I kept a fragmentary record of happenings which seemed, at the moment, to establish some point in the seasonal chronology. But the only result is a mad confusion. What is one to say of birds which begin to nest before even leaf buds have appeared on the deciduous trees, and what is one to do when it becomes very difficult to decide which is a last rose of summer, which a first flower of spring? Under such conditions, perhaps only the ornamental orange trees, putting forth blossoms while the old fruit still glows warmly on the branches, really make any sense.

The wildest disorder was certainly that prevailing

in the garden of an acquaintance, where the introduced plants attempted to conduct themselves in accordance with their old habit of responding to
warmth and moisture. There, last year's roses were
still blooming in early winter while this year's nar-
cissi were greeting a supposed spring in December.
But in wild nature, too, things were almost as con-
fusing. Even in December and even on a mountainside at four thousand feet, little spotted butterflies
flitted about in the sun while here and there some
member of the indefatigable Composite family con-
tinued to bloom and, within the shelter of a stone,
a scarlet mallow put forth a few last blossoms. In my
dooryard down below, a pair of cactus wrens was,
at the same moment, constructing a nest, though
even I knew enough not to take too seriously the activities of this fanatical builder who frequently con-
structs several unnecessary nests. Moreover, and to
do them justice, this particular pair did exercise so
much self-restraint that its young did not get out
into the world before May.

The fact remains nevertheless that their "procreant
cradle" was constructed before we had our depth of
winter—which last, as it happens, came and went
while I was on my two-week tour of inspection in
other deserts. Three inches of snow, they tell me, fell
during the night of January first and lay on the ground
until noon. It was the first precipitation of any kind

we had had in more than four months. Once again, after my return, there was a morning during which the ground was white for a few hours. Two days later, however, I was again strolling coatless in the sunshine; and a cat who has adopted me was rolling itself luxuriously on the ground, after the fashion of New England cats when they sense that the six-month winter has been broken.

Within a few weeks after that, various birds began to exhibit the symptoms of pleasant emotional disturbance. Two sparrow hawks who had long been keeping their solitary vigils at separate points of vantage took to sitting, at evening, side by side on a telephone wire. One of the large, bold thrashers who had never, even last June, uttered anything except his impudent whistle, suddenly burst into song. But when, on January 22, a female fluttered invitingly near, he behaved as though he thought this was rushing the season unduly. Then, in the middle of a long, sleepy afternoon late in the same month, I saw a mockingbird, sitting on the edge of my roof, do something which is no doubt common enough but which I do not remember ever having seen a bird do before. He yawned widely and with evident satisfaction. Nothing could have more perfectly typified that delightful disease, spring fever.

Almost imperceptibly, through February and early March, the pulse of the happy season beat fuller and stronger. Butterflies, once rather a rarity, became common. The first to appear in force were those same mourning cloaks, dark with a cream-colored border, which circle the temperate regions of the globe and are common in New England though rather rare in Britain, where the admiring natives know them as the Camberwell beauty. Exotics, like the zebra swallowtail uncommon or unknown farther north, appear only slightly later, and about the same time hummingbirds return from the south.

A neighbor, rather dubious about nature and rather inclined to resent her tooth and claw, told me indignantly that she had just seen a thrasher eat one of the newly arrived hummers. But for once I was able to console her. What the thrasher ate was only one of those moths which, like the related species in New England, do look and behave astonishingly like the mothlike bird. For some not very clear reason my neighbor agrees that this is not so bad and takes the thrasher back into her favor. That birds should eat insects is somehow an acceptable fact. I suggested that she should get a book on "How to Tell the Birds from the Bugs," in order to avoid in the future such painful mistakes; it would tell her which victims she ought to feel sorry for.

After careful consideration of the irreconcilable data I have come finally to the conclusion that the equinox is a time as suitable as any other to say "Spring is here." At least most of the birds who winter in Mexico or southward seem to think so. About that time the three visiting orioles—Bullock's, Scott's, and the hooded—put in their yellow-and-black appearance; about that time also, the vermilion flycatcher decided to act upon his opinion that the hunting would be good in this, for him, northerly clime. I saw him first at his post on the bare branch of a low shrub, his black back gleaming and his vermilion face, breast, and belly flaming in the sun. When he dived swiftly after some invisible insect, the red seemed actually fluorescent or self-lumious, and I agreed instantaneously with those who call him the most brilliant of all the birds found within the United States.

If the ornithologists are right in believing that the light of lengthening days is what puts birds on the move, then they cannot be much influenced by unseasonable freaks of the weather. With plants it is otherwise, and I imagine things were a bit delayed in that department by the fact that the showers we should have had in February did not come until late March. By the equinox, nevertheless, the improbable, and improbably bright, flowers which bloom by the driest desert roadsides were beginning to startle the eye by suddenly blazing forth where it had, only a short time before, appeared as though nothing could ever grow. Already in mid-February the wild rhubarb, a coarse weed, was putting forth its not overly attractive flower, but it hardly counted. Now, masses of purple verbena began to appear from nowhere; the prickly, foot-high shrub called false mesquite began to call attention to itself by displaying its purple, threadlike "fairy dusters," and the so-called desert marigold waved its innumerable, curiously luminous yellow heads in the sun. In New England, the earliest spring flowers are modest and retiring; here, they flaunt themselves, florally if not vegetatively, as conspicuously as August weeds do in the East.

Only one point seemed yet to be decided. What happens in ponds has always seemed to me of crucial importance for fixing the date of the pantheist's Easter, and there were no ponds or anything like ponds in my immediate vicinity. But where there are mountains in addition to desert there will be almost every conceivable variety of physical environment, and so I made an inspection of the canyon, some fifteen miles away, down which a small stream flows at certain seasons, leaving behind it little pools not destined to disappear entirely even during the driest parts of the year. The cottonwoods which follow the course of the stream were already greenish; along their trunks, the lizards were sunning them-

selves; and by the margins of the pools, various mois-
ture-loving plants were already flourishing.

In the water itself, all the features of the New England miracle were repeating themselves. At my approach, frogs leaped into the water already swarming
with tadpoles; a crayfish hid himself between two
submerged rocks; a garter snake crawled out to sun
himself on a stone.

A few months before, on my last previous visit, the
water haunts had seemed as lifeless as those of New
England from November to March. No change of
temperature seems sufficient to account for this sudden awakening into life, but the Rites of Spring were
being celebrated as enthusiastically as they are celebrated in regions where there seems to be more of
stern reality, less of mere ritual, in this resurrection
from the dead. Perhaps the actual cause is the disappearance of the cool nights, which had warned
all sleeping creatures that the morning of the year had
not yet arrived. Perhaps, for all I know, many of the
creatures merely want their winter sleep whether
there is any winter or not—just as Eskimos go to bed
in the summer even though the sun is shining, or as
the inhabitants of Havana change from linen clothes
to wool in December merely because they do not
want to be deprived by perpetual summer of their
right to a variety of garments.

But I shall not inquire too closely into physical determinants. I like to think that a renewal and a rebirth are natural even where the whole earth does not die a deep death. What happens here is not so dramatic as the events elsewhere, but none of the denizens of any part of the dry land is totally deprived of the experience. If the time should ever come when I find myself a permanent resident here, I think the Lower Sonoran spring would be quite sufficient for the indispensible purposes of ritual.

Moreover, if some drama is absent from some aspects of the local spring, the visible presence of high mountains only a few miles away guarantees certain theatrical spectacles which furnish considerable compensation. On May third, low clouds covered the sky, a heavy shower flooded the desert, and a curtain of mist covered the mountains almost to their bases. Next morning, when it lifted, they were white with snow. In three-quarters of an hour by car I was in a pine forest where the boughs were bent under their burden of snow; returning, I ran into a sleetstorm which whitened the road. Yet at the house, when I got back, the sun was shining brightly and the temperature was in the seventies. No wonder that both plant and animal life here is sharply zoned in a fashion which delights the hearts of ecologists. Many a plant, bird, and animal sticks almost as closely to his altitude belt as though he were on an island surrounded by water instead of merely in an environment determined by his height above sea level.

Now that mid-May has arrived, there is not likely to be even in the mountains, any more winter, and here below spring has passed into summer. The omnipresent prickly pears, which grew thin and discouraged during the seven-month drought, grew plump again after the first real shower and are covered with the large, lemon-colored flowers which will presently give way to luscious-looking, purple fruits in incredible numbers. These the Indians used to eat and in eastern cities one sometimes sees them exposed for sale in the more luxurious fruit stores. But they look, I must confess, more luscious than they taste—as I discovered last summer when on an idle afternoon I collected a bushel from one plant and turned them into a beautiful red syrup to be added to cool drinks. It was as good as grenadine in taste as well as in color; but that is such mild praise that on the whole I considered my experiment in smoking the common wild tobacco of the region rather more successful.

Other, smaller cacti are also blooming, and so are the giant saguaros, at the ends of whose grotesquely curving arms there appear little circlets of creamy white flowers. The effect is modestly pretty but seems

a little inadequate for so gigantic a plant; and it
suggests the odd fact that in the cactus family there
seems to be a strange lack of proportion between the
size of the various species and the size of the blossoms
they bear. The saguaro flower is smaller than that of
the prickly pear; even more remarkable, many a
five- or six-inch variety, half-hidden under a shrub
or a stone, bears flowers as large or larger than either.
One hardly notices these plants until they bloom; and
one would hardly notice the bloom on the saguaro
had not the forty- or fifty-foot trunk long been the
most conspicuous thing in the landscape.

These monsters are almost the trade-mark of
Arizona and their blossoms are its official "state
flower." That is understandable enough, both because the giants are absolutely unique in the vegetable world and also because they are, practically
speaking, Arizona's exclusive possession since, except
for a few negligible stands in California, they grow
nowhere else north of the border. Nevertheless, if I
had to choose one plant to express the spirit of the
Sonoran Desert—one which combines oddness of
form and habit with the courage to flourish under
seemingly impossible conditions, and which combines also the defensive fierceness of thorns with the
spectacular, unexpected beauty of brilliant flowers
—I think I should choose the ocotillo.

This spectacular shrub, sometimes appropriately called slimwood and coachwhip, is officially *Fouquieria splendens* and is the only representative of its genus and family in the United States. Its unbranched, almost straight stems, sometimes as many as fifteen or twenty of them, radiate from the common center at ground level and often reach ten or twelve feet into the air. Standing a few feet apart, they frequently dominate many acres of their preferred desert slopes, which they have claimed so successfully that one is aware of little else. The long wands, an inch or more thick and colored a soft gray faintly tinged with green, are composed of wood so dense, so hard, and so tough that the Papago Indians still use them for palisades; yet in the light breeze they nod just sufficiently to avoid any suggestion of stiffness as they stand, most of the time bare of leaves, waiting patiently for their moments. Yet only the very unobservant would think them dead. Even in the stillest air of the hottest midday a certain springiness or resilience which is the very essence of life somehow expresses itself clearly.

After any substantial shower which happens to fall at almost any time of the year, hundreds of very small leaves spring directly from the wands along their entire lengths and clothe them in a sort of layer of green too thin to obscure their outline. For a week or two these leaves go actively about their business of turning carbon dioxide into the carbohydrate of plant tissues; then, when the soil has ceased to supply the moisture which the plant cannot afford any longer to lose by evaporation, the leaves drop off to appear again a few months later, so that, in the course of a year, the ocotillo may enjoy not one but four or five separate springs and autumns.

Nevertheless, it knows somehow when the one authentic spring has come and, whether it be at the moment leafy or leafless, a tapering cluster of buds forms at the very tip of nearly every branch and soon expands into a four- or five-inch cone of waxy scarlet blossoms. Over many a bare slope otherwise almost completely destitute of bright color, hundreds of these little flames are waved gently back and forth in the breeze until it is hard not to believe, literally, the inevitable description—hundreds of torches mysteriously burning across the desert as far as sight can reach. Seen as one often sees them, the tips against the deep blue of an Arizona sky, the effect is as surprising and as festive as anything in nature.

Ever since midwinter I have had my eye on a wonderful stretch of desert tucked away in a valley among the lowest foothills of a mountain range; when I judged that the ocotillos would be in full flame I sought it out again. Except for the cabin of a forest ranger a mile or two away, there was no human habitation less than four or five miles distant: except for my one companion and the lizards which scampered about everywhere, I had the whole torch-lighted world to myself, and that included a great deal more than the dominant torches themselves. It was near summer by now; we had had our delayed showers and every living thing had responded. Though the prickly pear, also in yellow bloom, was the only other large plant seriously to dispute with the ocotillos for possession of the land, there were scores of humbler organisms able to find their niches. Tucked away between stones, the little echinocereus cacti were shaded under the absurd opulence of their large purple flowers, and, by way of variety, there was an area of desert floor a few hundred yards away which looked just as dry as the rest but which must have been somehow more favorably situated in some respect since it was covered by a bright, variegated carpet of tiny plants.

Many of them were annuals and most looked like the little alpines of some cultivated rock garden. Within an area of a few square yards I counted some fifteen different species, all in bloom. Most had almost no foliage and seemed to consist almost exclusively of blossoms. Such vegetative parts as they had were either threadlike, or fuzzy, or dry, for they were all determined to waste no moisture. Yet many of the blossoms are recognizable as desert cousins of familiar flowers. This delicately pale yellow one is, by its form and structure, obviously related to the blue, rankly growing wild lettuce of the East, though the stem is only a few inches instead of several feet high. That tiny pink one is unmistakably a houstonia or bluet; even more evidently, this other is a dwarf delphinium. Most of the annuals will be dead within a few weeks, after having rushed from dormant seed to dormant seed again before the scanty moisture is all gone. A few of the perennials may bloom again after the summer rains; the others will have left seeds to lie inactive for perhaps nine months before they germinate in their turn. Since this was an unusually dry spring I probably saw none except the least demanding sorts, but I know that there are some which will tolerate only the wetter seasons and whose seeds, therefore, sometimes lie in the ground for several years until a relatively rainy spring comes around again.

On postcards and in travel magazines such scenes as this are usually labeled "Devil's Garden." But I see nothing infernal about it. Even the sentimental admit that every rose has its thorn, and they should be willing to admit that here every thorn is accompanied by its rose. Persistent legends notwithstanding, the cholla is not a "jumping cactus," and its joints do not detach themselves from the plant to leap at inoffensive passers-by. He who finds thorns in his arm or leg has certainly been, however inadvertently, the aggressor. The rudeness of the cactus, like that of Dr. Johnson, is a defensive rudeness. Its motto is only the motto of South Carolina: "Do not tread upon me."

When a wild animal is described as vicious, it usually means only that if you try to kill him he will sometimes defend himself. Those of us who do not consider this evidence of notable wickedness should not find it difficult to understand a cactus. When ranch visitors amuse themselves by lassoing the saguaros and pull over a giant which has been a century and a half in growing, that is merely another illustration of the fact that of all living creatures man is the most dangerous—to everything else that lives, as well as to himself.

Perhaps I am still a little bit romantic about the desert and therefore like best of all these "devil's gardens" because they represent the desert way of life in its most characteristic and most successful form. I have noticed, nevertheless, that even those permanent residents who love this country are inclined to form little oases about their houses and to pamper with the water from their wells some of the lusher forms of vegetation. Perhaps, after a time, the natural desert comes to seem too strenuous and too difficult for human nature's daily food, something to be contemplated for stimulation rather than lived with in one's more relaxed moments. It may be that in time I should come to feel the same way. But for the present I still find a cactus or an ocotillo very good company. I respect their virtues and they are indifferent to my weaknesses.

# Chapter Fourteen

## A Bird in the Bush

# A Bird in the Bush

Will Cuppy once remarked that the ability to distinguish one kind of sparrow from another was a gift which seemed to be hereditary in certain New England families. Not belonging to such a family, I am not surprised that I am not at all good at this particular art, science, or diversion. Nevertheless, I have long been a little ashamed that a professed lover of most animal creatures should know as little as I did about the birds. Many people begin, indeed many people also stop, with them. But a turtle or a lizard, even an unfamiliar bug, was surer to get my sympathetic attention. I knew by sight and sound the commoner birds of the lawns and gardens, but that was almost all.

For this perversity I have offered myself various excuses. For one thing, the birds seemed determined to elude me. They were always flying away or hiding behind leaves when I wanted to see what they looked like. Old-fashioned bird lovers, like Audubon, used to blaze away with a gun when this situation arose, and some still do. But I have a sentimental disinclination to shoot a passer-by just to find out who he is. In fact, once he was dead I don't think I should very much care. And so the birds and I went about our respective business.

Moreover, the loss was, I think, exclusively mine since there is probably some truth as well as some exaggeration in the opinion recently expressed in print that—when all the "collecting," photographing, and experimentation is taken into consideration—the best friend of the birds is often the one who pays no attention to them. A winter handout of suet and seeds is no doubt often appreciated, but what starts that way often ends quite differently.

Had I stayed at home in New England I should perhaps never have made a start. One does not like to begin learning one's letters at fifty and more. But in a new environment ignorance is nothing to be ashamed of. All the commoner birds which haunt the open desert itself—thrashers, cactus wrens, white-winged doves, road-runners and Gambel's quail—thrust themselves upon my attention. They appreciated the dish of water I put out for their benefit; they got into the habit of paying me regular visits; and there were no leaves for them to hide behind.

Nothing so difficult as sparrow-distinguishing was called for, and at least this company of a dozen regular visitors was soon as familiar as the robin and catbird. Armed with one of the modern field guides which are so much better adapted to the needs of the beginner than the old bird books used to be, I was soon wandering down the canyons, along the washes, and even into the pine forests of the higher mountains, looking for species which have no great fondness for the cactus and the sand. Before I knew it, I was equipped with a better pair of binoculars than I had ever owned before and, murmuring an occasional apology to Thoreau who boasted that he was well along in life before he consented to use a "spy glass," I was engaged in that sometimes ridiculed enterprise called "compiling a life list."

This game, which consists merely in seeing how many different birds one can identify, is played on the side by some "serious" ornithologists, but it is also often despised both by the ultrascientific on the one hand and by the ultrapoetical or philosophical on the other. The more advanced form, which consists in keeping the score for a year or even a single hectic day, has been derisively called "ornithogolf," but it is at least harmless even to the birds, most of whom do not seem to mind being peered at through binoculars. Simple listing seems to me rather more like stamp collecting than like golf, but as long as one competes with nobody except oneself it affords the elementary pleasures associated with "making a collection" of anything. One is easily pleased with one's own achievements as long as no anxious comparisons are made, and what does not grow very fast at least never goes backward.

I felt quite pleased when my list had reached forty, though now that it numbers one hundred and thirty-eight—including a few California species—I look back with tolerant amusement upon the ignorant satisfaction of a few months ago. For an eastern community, one hundred and thirty-eight would be quite good for a tyro; but it is less impressive out here, where the number of different birds is much greater. In the entire United States there are said to be about six hundred and fifty species. A census taken by a group one Christmas day turned up one hundred and seventeen within a circle fifteen miles in diameter with its center at Tucson. A similar count at Brownsville, Texas, yielded one hundred and sixty-four. And since I have wandered over a much larger area and also had the advantage of a whole cycle of the seasons, my record would not interest the virtuosos—among whom are such prodigies as Ludlow Griscom who is said to be able to recognize five hundred birds by their songs alone. But I am not competing with anyone except that dead self which thought forty quite a respectable number.

Fortunately for such as I, a surprising number of the southwestern birds are bright-colored and strikingly distinctive. We, too, have our sparrows; but many of them are quite easy to tell apart, and the more difficult ones are not necessary to fill out a respectably long list. Moreover, if my collection has not done anything else for me, it led to the discovery of a charming nook I would probably not otherwise have found.

In his admirable *Birds Over America* Roger Tory Peterson mentions a certain Carr Canyon in the Huachuca Mountains which run just north of the Mexican border in southeastern Arizona. This range is a happy but imperfectly exploited hunting ground for naturalists, both because various Mexican birds, plants, and animals get just that far north and because the abrupt heights rising rapidly from the hot desert to the pine forests of a Canadian Zone include within a very short linear distance an extraordinary number of "life zones." Many creatures, some probably still undescribed, are to be found there and nowhere else in the United States.

This Carr Canyon, so Mr. Peterson thought, was the most interesting place of all for birds. Someday, he says, he would like to rent from Major Healey, who runs a cattle ranch there, the little cottage part way up the canyon which was built many years ago by a naturalist named Biedermann who chose that remote spot to pass his last years after he had retired from service in the United States Biological Survey.

Now though Carr Canyon is not on the road maps, those of the Geological Survey know it well. It turned out to be very easily accessible, and it was a simple matter to make arrangements with the affable Major and his bird-loving wife. In no time at all my companion and I were in possession of Biedermann's cottage which, as I later discovered, has been at one time or another occupied by various of my betters.

The cottage is tucked away in a corner of the canyon at an elevation of fifty-five hundred feet and less than a mile from the ranch house. But it is also just at the foot of towering cliffs reaching up another fifteen hundred feet or so to the level of the Canyon's head, though still a good twenty-five hundred below the nine thousand five hundred foot summit of the neighboring Miller Peak. Biedermann died there alone in 1932, at the age of ninety-three; he is buried a few hundred yards away up the canyon under a suitable pile of stones most unsuitably marked by a little horseshoe-shaped metal plaque lying loosely on the stones. This plaque does bear the name and dates, but these are much less conspicuous than the

name and address of the "funeral directors" who
supplied it and were obviously less anxious that the
visitor should remember Biedermann than that, if he
should have any business in their line, he should know
where to find them.

Hurrying back to the cottage it was a relief to get
a contrasting reminder that what had interested those
old bones in life was still going on. Under the eaves
I had discovered a last year's nest of the blue-throated
hummingbird, largest of the American hummers. The
owner, I had been told, was due back soon from Mexico, and I saw what I think was her first visit of inspection. She flew around the corner of the house, poised
in the air to look the nest over, dropped into it for
a few seconds to try it for fit, and then perched for a
while on a wire before flying away—apparently satisfied that only a little redecorating was necessary.

In the cottage itself I found also a translation of
Tacitus' *Germania*, with many passages underlined.
I do not know to whom it had belonged but in the
absence of information to the contrary I shall assume
that the old man meditated during the evenings on
this testimony to the ancient virtues of his race. In the
same volume was the same author's *History*, containing a sentence which must have been the source of
Milton's "last infirmity of noble mind," and was certainly an appropriate subject for thought on the part
of one who had chosen to spend his last years so far

out of what is called the world. "The desire of glory clings even to the best of men longer than any other passion."

Around the cottage, deer and wild turkeys were a common sight; though I never caught sight of the little nocturnal wild pig called javelina or peccary, I nosed him one night just outside the door where his odor—"double skunk" would be a good description of it—overpowered everything. Neither, I regret to say, did I see in the wild a troop of coatis, though Mrs. Healey had as ranchyard pet an orphan raised on canned milk and baby food.

These exotic creatures, which seem as though they had no business outside a tropical jungle, look a little like monkeys and a little like badgers. But despite their short hair, they are said to be more closely related to the raccoon than to any other North American mammal. They belong in South and Central America and also in Mexico and until a comparatively few years ago, they were never known in this country. Recently, however, they have been extending their range, just as the possum has been extending his in New England, and are said to be rather common along a narrow strip just north of the border.

The only one with which I am intimately acquainted—he jumped into my lap before I knew what he was—is about the size of a small dog. He has

a pointed, mobile snout which he uses to hunt for
insects in the ground and a thirty-inch tail—nearly as
long as his body—which he carries either straight out
or straight up, depending on mood, and which looks
prehensile but isn't. He lopes about the yard with a
curiously agile gait despite the fact that his flat hind
feet contribute an incongruously lumbering, bearlike
roll to his movement. He is up the trees, onto the roof,
and continuously into everything, with the mischiev-
ousness of a monkey and a monkey's determination
to tease the tolerant dogs who tussle with him when
they feel like it and drive him away with angry barks
when they don't.

Chula—which means "cute"—is the Mexican name.
Like a coon, he seems to be, with strangers, a little
forgetful of the sharpness of his playful bite, but he
cuddles in his mistress' arms like a kitten and permits
himself to be carried about by his strong tail. I
should guess that he is just about grown-up now, and
I asked Mrs. Healey how she proposed to keep him if
the time came when he began to feel the desire for
the company of other chulas. Her reply was wiser
than that usually given by the keepers of wild pets:
"If he wants to stay he can stay; if he wants to go he
can go."

As for the birds I came to see, they flocked about
in such numbers as almost to defeat the principal ra-

tional excuse for birding—that it takes one on long walks. Less than a hundred yards from the ranch house there is a little clump of trees and under them a thin trickle of water from a well. In arid country birds must pay regular visits to such spots, just as the animals in the jungle must come to water holes, and if one is content to sit slothfully in a chair, the majority of all the species of the region will come.

Within three minutes, a hermit thrush and a black-headed grosbeak, accompanied by the pileolated, Audubon's and Townsend's warblers came to drink. Five minutes before, a lazuli bunting and a Bullock's oriole had been there together, and to see such brilliantly contrasting birds a few inches apart gives one almost the impression of being in a bird store rather than a remote fastness of the mountains. In a few hours, without moving from the chair, I saw also cedar waxwings, the red and yellow western tanager, the red-backed junco, the cañon towhee, the yellow warbler, Virginia's warbler, and various other less spectacular or more familiar birds. On other days there were other warblers as well as other species, large and small, including the quaint bridled titmouse found in the United States only among the mountains of southern Arizona and southern New Mexico. An ornithologist making a census found one hundred and seven species on the ranch itself.

The ranch house sits at the foot of the canyon, whose head lies high up in the mountains. To follow the canyon itself would involve, so I was told, very rough going indeed. But in the spring the cattle are taken up by a circuitous route to browse in the mountains. A car can negotiate a primitive road and from its end one can walk down into the canyon's upper end. Up there, in a sheltered pine forest, a different race of birds, some of whom never visit the lower region, takes over, and pine siskins breed there as they do in Canada.

Twice I made the trip, partly to see what new could be added to the list, partly just because the armchair existence by the water hole seemed too ignominious. It was odd to see on the heights a little brown creeper almost identical with that of New England; and the journey yielded, besides, one bright little mite never seen in the United States except high up in the mountains near the corner where Arizona, New Mexico, and old Mexico meet. It was the red-faced warbler, a tiny black-and-white bird with a splash of bright red on his face and breast. Only a week or two later I might have seen, down below, the coppery-tailed trogon, perhaps the most famous of the aliens who overstep the international boundaries. I didn't see him, but if I should ever become a really passionate bird collector he would be something to live for.

Of one thing, moreover, this little stay in the Huachucas made me even surer than before. *A bird in the bush is worth two in the hand.* It is also worth two dozen or two hundred dozen in the benzene-drenched trays over which taxonomists, secure in the conviction that they are the only "serious" ornithologists, spend their lives.

Despite the grand mystery of migration, birds are not, in certain senses, very interesting animals. They have, so one kind of scientist is very anxious to insist, small reptilian brains; and even their consciousness, if they have any, is far more different from ours than that of the humblest mammal. Unlike the even remoter insects, their behavior patterns are relatively simple and, in the various species, relatively repetitious. Any sense we may have of an emotional identification with them is largely fictitious. They are not so much fellow creatures as aesthetic objects on the one hand, and symbols on the other. We notice them first because they are brightly colored and move quickly; if they come to exercise any fascination stronger than that produced by these simple facts, it is because they seem so free from our physical and emotional limitations. "As free as the birds of the air" is an inevitable simile. But it is only a simile. Between them and us there is no real analogy possible. They stimulate our imaginations but there is not really anything we can learn from them. And for that reason a dead bird is simply not a bird any more. The bubble is pricked, the illusion vanished. What had interested us was not bones and feathers but an idea.

The contemporary school of field ornithologists is aware of this. To an astonishing degree the binocular and the camera have replaced the gun in the equipment of the student. Many such would hesitate, as Audubon did not, to shoot a hundred specimens of a newly discovered bird just to observe to what extent dimensions or feather patterns seem to vary. But the taxonomists, having for all practical purposes come to the end of available American species to classify, have invented the concept of "subspecificity," and now enjoy the endless possibilities involved in the establishment of local "races" of robins, chickadees, or what not, for the doubtful determination of which vast series of corpses must be collected and filed away in the dismal basements of museums.

It is also a little startling to read in Peterson's *Birds Over America* what happened when an apparently extinct bird was rediscovered in 1886. The bird in question was Bachman's warbler, which Audubon first described from a specimen killed near Charleston in 1833. It was not officially reported again until 1886; but during the next few years a flood of corpses reached the museums, and at least one hundred and sixty-seven were shot. "Today," says Peterson without further comment, "I do not know a man in America who can show me a Bach-man's warbler." Quite obviously, in other words, there are still a good many people "interested in birds" who would rather have a given species extinct than insufficiently represented in the study trays of the museums. No less obviously, therefore, there is sound sense in Mr. Cuppy's advice to the ivory-billed woodpecker: "Keep away from bird lovers, fellows, or you'll be standing on a little wooden pedestal containing your full name in Latin."

In all fairness it must be admitted that, except possibly in the case of birds already near extinction, the collecting done by taxonomists probably does not decrease the bird population. Since Peterson wrote the lament above even Bachman's warbler has been seen again and so may have escaped the bird lovers. Birds are very prolific and the natural death rate is very high. The draining of swamps and the clearing of forests, which deprives some species of a suitable environment and sometimes simultaneously provides others with new areas to colonize, is a more important factor than deliberate killing. Moreover, there is re-spectable authority behind the opinion that neither small boys with air rifles nor the much maligned cat have actually been responsible for reducing the total number of birds in the United States because other, more effectual limiting factors would have kept it down to the present level even if boys and cats had both been liquidated. The fact remains, nevertheless, that as deliberate killers the taxonomists stand high, and that while the Audubon societies try to impress the school children with the sacredness of life the "serious students" get their licenses to "collect" hundreds of specimens. When a specialist decides to "undertake the revision" of a genus, that is very bad news indeed for the individuals who have the misfortune to belong in it. If they had their say, they would much prefer to remain in that confusion into which, so the specialists would assure them, the question of the number of authentic subspecies has recently fallen.

Thoreau thought that being an inspector of snowstorms was a sufficient occupation for one man, but we are a serious people and only a few eccentrics can satisfy their consciences if they just go about looking at birds. Most who go in for ornithology have to "do something about them" and, if classifying isn't enough, then, like the modern students of everything else, they take up "problems."

In the old days and in England you could get yourself quite a reputation by imploring a skylark to:

> Teach me half the gladness
> That thy brain must know. . . .

But no amount of "harmonious madness" flowing from the lips of a graduate student would win him a Ph.D.

Moreover, in ornithology, as in the other sciences, the preferred problems are those which are stated (and of course therefore also solved) in mechanistic terms. The result is that by the time a serious ornithologist has got done with a bird that bird is not much more interesting than Man himself seems to be after the sociologists and the behaviorists have done a good job explaining *his* behavior. In both cases, statistics are now the favorite tool. An individual bird, like an individual man, becomes only a card with certain holes punched in it. Neither he nor the card is, by itself, of any significance. But if you get a lot of cards, put the whole stack into one of the contraptions manufactured by International Business Machines, and then turn the switch, wisdom will come out at the other end.

To many temperaments, including mine, righteous indignation is a very uncomfortable emotion and should not be cultivated in connection with situations which do not imperatively call for it. Being just back from a delightful, outrageously irresponsible, and dilettantish two weeks of watching the birds of the air, what I really feel in connection with the earnest classifier and the earnest dealer in problems is not indignation but a certain pity. In many cases, no doubt, he got into the thing because he too saw birds as aesthetic objects and as symbols. Probably he chose his profession because he had some vision of himself spending his life out of doors, rejoicing in the sense of freedom which the sight of a bird generated in him. Probably also he does not quite know how it happened that he is, instead, breathing insecticide rather than fresh air and handling dried skins which would certainly not be interesting to anyone to whom they did not remotely suggest the living things which once they were. It is no wonder that he "compensates" by affecting a scorn of all concerned in less "scientific" pursuits.

I am resolved, even, to be grateful to him for such of his labors as help to make possible the handbooks from which I have learned the little I know about how to tell one bird from another. But I shall also chuckle when I find that a taxonomist so redoubtable in his own line as William Morton Wheeler was ready to take my point of view. "It quite saddens me," he wrote, "to think that when I cross the Styx I may find myself among so many professional biologists condemned to keep on trying to solve problems, and that Pluto, or whoever is in charge down there, may condemn me to sit forever trying to identify specimens from my own specific and generic diagnoses, while the amateur entomologists, who have not been damned professors, are permitted to roam at will among the fragrant asphodels of the Elysian meadows, netting gorgeous, ghostly butterflies until the end of time."

*Chapter Fifteen*

Undiscovered Country

# Undiscovered Country

In the good old days, it took thirteen to make a baker's dozen. Under our economy of abundance, such amiable cheats have, paradoxically, pretty well disappeared. But a sabbatical year still means fifteen months for a few of the more fortunate college professors.

When twelve of mine had passed, it seemed a good idea to spend a part of the dividend or lagniappe away from home, in that high region of sandstone buttes where, years ago, I first felt the fascination of the Southwest's lonely grandeur. Just returned from a seventeen-hundred-mile circuit, my eyes have not yet recovered from the merciless assault of bright colors and bold forms, but I know that memory had not deceived me. There is probably no spot on earth where inanimate nature makes a more stunning display of one special kind of overwhelming magnificence.

Once the southern wall of that plateau which covers almost the whole northern half of Arizona has been climbed, a different world appears. For one thing, the altitudes range from about five thousand to more than twelve thousand feet; for another, the topography and the geology are predominantly different. Between the peaks, the most characteristic features are no longer the unbroken expanses of cactus and creosote desert but recent formations of red and white sandstone eroded by wind and water into deep, sheer-walled canyons and isolated "monuments," sometimes a thousand feet high, which stand like the abandoned cities of some race of prehistoric giants. By comparison, the Sonoran Desert seems cozy. Here the earth defies man to live upon it, and for the most part he has not challenged the defiance.

In the few miles which lie between the south rim of the plateau and the gash cut by the Colorado River the land is still definitely inhabited, but north of the river a region extending well into southeastern Utah is emptier than most Americans imagine any part of their country to be. Only here and there on the Navajo Reservation an Indian family has built a hogan in the shadow of a monument, and manages miraculously to raise a few sheep from whose wool a woman weaves her blanket on a loom set up in the sand. Off the reservation, it is only here and there that a few farmers, mostly Mormons, have taken advantage of an occasional small stream to establish a homestead, or to run their cattle over vast areas where the beasts manage to find some "browse" though grass is nearly nonexistent.

This region is isolated from the north by stretches of seldom-traversed desert in Utah; isolated from the south by the Colorado River which, except for the mule bridge at the bottom of the Grand Canyon, is uncrossable for the hundreds of miles which lie between Navajo Bridge and Lake Mead. Within the region itself there are a few tiny communities to serve the needs of the Indians and ranchers; some of them are connected by good roads, while others lie along meandering routes from which all except the most experienced travelers are warned off. Finally, in the desert to the north, there are hundreds of square miles, roadless and broken, into which no human being wanders for months, perhaps for years, at a time.

For a certain kind of traveler, such a region as this offers unique advantages. On the one hand, it is not far away, as the wild places of the earth go, for it can be reached from a center of population in the short space of a day or two. On the other hand, once

one has got into it, one could hardly feel more remote anywhere in the world, and it offers a nicely
graded series of adventures for the timid hardly to
be equaled elsewhere. Without leaving the broad
highway, the inexperienced can visit Grand Canyon;
then, if they find rather too many other people star-
ing into that stupendous gully, much as they stare
at an excavation in New York City, they can turn off
into the sand at, say, a point just ten miles north of
Cameron, and within half an hour find themselves in
what will appear a trackless wilderness. Next time,
grown a little bolder, they may strike a little deeper;
and if the time comes when even the most primitive
road seems to spoil the effect, they can find someone
familiar with the country who will lead them into
places which, in actual fact, have been trod by few
human feet.

Not many of us, when seized by the desire to know
what the lonely places are like, can afford an expedition to the Gobi. But no great resources of either
money or daring are necessary to get what must be a
good deal the same effect somewhere in either the
Arizona Strip or the even lonesomer country in southeastern Utah. It is literally "white on the map." Here
is adventure without danger and the opportunity for
many an expedition upon which even the not very
rugged can dare to embark. It is not likely that I, at
least, will ever undertake anything more sensational,

and though it is not enough to make one a figure at the Explorers Club I have heard rumors that not all safaris are actually very much more difficult.

Even the main highway which leads north to the Navajo Bridge and ultimately on to Salt Lake City is a memorable experience for those who discover it for the first time. Like several other of the main arteries in the West and unlike any in the East, it justifies the conduct of those obsessed travelers who pause for nothing and seem intent only on making their four or five hundred miles a day. That other automobiles are likely to be five miles rather than fifty feet apart encourages high speed, but the spaces traversed are so wide, so open, and so vast that the strongest determination to see nothing is defeated and the great features of the landscape remain fixed in their places no matter how frantically the wheels turn.

This is not a country of separate "views," visible only from some point of vantage, but a panorama which cannot be made to pass other than slowly. One does not look at a landscape, one passes through it, and in no other that I have ever seen is the pure sensation of space so beautiful or so overwhelming. It is continuously a vivid reality, and for once the automobilist's tendency to hurry should be encouraged because in no other way will he realize so strongly that this is what he cannot do, that here, where sixty miles an hour is almost standing still,

one begins to understand how it can be that in inter-
planetary space a hundred times faster is still nothing at all.

Resting some years ago at the summit of Navajo
Mountain, which rises ten thousand feet just north of
the Arizona border and up whose sides no road has
ever been attempted, I looked down upon an area of
stony, broken plateau which included, so I was told,
an area as large as Connecticut but inhabited by no
single man, white or Indian. For all I know, this may
have been a slight exaggeration; for I have since
learned from observation how persistently isolated
settlers push themselves in from around the edges of
uninhabited areas to take up lonely residence, sometimes in places fantastically inaccessible to the outside
world. In any event, nevertheless, this is one of the few
remaining "white spots" on the map of the United
States, and much of it may fairly be called unexplored.
Parties have traversed it from time to time, and there
are a few recognized routes which follow tracks, sometimes passable to cars with four-wheel drives, sometimes not. It was through this area that in 1776 Father
Escalante tried to make his way from Santa Fe to
California and had such bad luck that few have since
tried his route. One would have to travel far to find another area less well known or, for that matter, one

which until now has offered fewer reasons other than aesthetic ones why anyone should want to know it.

In its own aloof, almost contemptuous, way it is nevertheless extraordinarily beautiful—nature's ultimate achievement in that Southwestern Style which surprisingly executes great monolithic forms, sometimes sculptural and sometimes architectural, in bright, multihued sandstone. About the style there is nothing to suggest the charm of the landscape which welcomes man; instead, there is only the grandeur of something powerfully alien, indifferent, and enduring, as though it had been made to please the eye and perhaps even to soothe the spirit of some creature older, as well as less transitory, than he. Ever since I got my Pisgah sight of it stretching away several thousand feet below the mountain, I have hoped some day to penetrate at least a little way into the almost unviolated fastnesses. And now I have done so.

One spectacular section was first "discovered" three or four years ago. The quotes I use for a reason to be presently apparent, but at least photographs were then first taken for publication and it became a region where one might with a minimum of effort become, if not a Balboa, then at least a pilgrim sufficiently early to feel that he had escaped the shame of being a mere vulgar sight-seer. There is nothing that a tourist despises more than another tourist, and Cathedral Valley, as it was promptly dubbed, is not yet on any tourist route.

The jumping-off-place is Fremont, one of those surprising little communities due to the enterprise of the Mormons who industriously colonized every fertile spot. Fremont is only a few miles from a paved road; it has one telephone for the general use of the inhabitants and a power line connected with some hydroelectric plant far away. But it is also sixty miles from the nearest doctor or dentist, and from its eastern edge the great white area stretches away. I found there the descendant of an early settler who knew the country, was possessed of a jeep, and readily persuadable to show me a region which he, unlike many natives of remote places, found absorbingly interesting. Within fifteen minutes after I had first laid eyes upon him we were off.

An ungraded road used by cattlemen leads up a mountainside to a minor summit something over eight thousand feet high. From it one looks north toward a higher peak, which was still, in June, snow-clad at the top, its slopes clothed in aspens, some already in leaf, others, in the less-favored areas, not yet green. To the south, at one's feet, begins a panorama which seems totally unrelated to any other part of the landscape. The mountain falls precipitously away for several thousand feet and from its base there stretches, as far as the eye can reach, a desert floor shimmering in the hot sun. Here and there plateaus, miles long and miles broad, rise almost sheer from the flatlands. Between them, the floor is sprinkled with sandstone buttes, larger than any man-built cathedral, which sometimes suggest Perpendicular Gothic, sometimes the Angkor Wat. Inevitably the impression is of an abandoned city, vaster than any city, ancient or modern, ever was. We negotiated the descent, and after a final plunge down a forty-five degree angle, were upon the trackless floor itself, free to spend a long day circling the most impressive monuments, and in the process, gaining in respect for the capabilities of the jeep what we lost in that for the ability of the human body to absorb the bounces and the jerks incident to travel in a vehicle which—due allowance being made for its breadth—can go most places a horse can go.

In the course of that long day we saw no other human being, and had no reason to suppose that any other would come there within any particular period of time. It is thus truly a region uninhabited. But whether it is also "undiscovered" or even "recently discovered" is a different question, and others more competent than I have struggled with the attempt to define that much-abused term.

Vilhjalmur Stefansson's somewhat cynical formulation is perhaps as good as any. A country, he remarks, is generally said to be "discovered" when for the first time a white man—preferably an English-man—happens to set foot upon it. After all, it was only in that sense that Columbus "discovered" America, and few places except the Poles have ever been discovered in any other. What we really mean by the word is usually "made known to that part of the world to which we happen to belong," and in that sense Cathedral Valley really was "discovered" only a few years ago. But our guide—a strict Mormon who refused tea and coffee, as well as tobacco—was also an honest man and he volunteered the information that for at least fifty years a rancher had been turning his cattle loose in the "undiscovered" valley for the winter and rounding them up again when the time came for their summer on the mountain.

Perhaps "unseen" would be a better word than "undiscovered." That term can be made to stick, for the guide told us also that when he showed the first photographs to the cowboys they expressed astonishment as well as interest. "Where on earth is that?" And when they were assured that they had been there a score of times, they admitted that, perhaps, they had. But cowboys are interested in the state of their cattle and the state of their range, not very much interested in scenery, no matter how sublime. Hence they had not "discovered" the valley, either for the rest of the world or even for themselves.

According to a theory at least as old as Immanuel Kant a purely aesthetic experience is possible only in the presence of something which provokes no reaction other than contemplation. Thus a picture, no matter how realistic, differs from the object which it represents because the object invites us, as the picture does not, to act in connection with it. And though it seems unlikely that any of these cowbows had read the *Critique of Practical Reason* they certainly confirmed Kant's theory. When they saw Cathedral Valley itself they performed the activities which it suggested. Only when they saw a picture did they discover the thing itself because, for the first time, they then engaged in that contemplation which alone can make us aware of things-in-themselves. Since I had no cattle to tend and not even a horse or a jeep to manage I was free to treat the valley as an object of contemplation and it was for that I had come.

In no country remotely resembling it have I ever settled down to live, even for a week or two at a time. Now that I have returned to a different desert, which was never so strange to me as the one I had just left, the incredible valley seems more than far away— rather as though it were part of some universe discontinuous with this one and as inaccessible as the fourth dimension. Having treated it as nothing but an object of contemplation, it has already lost all reality except that of a work of the artistic imagination, and I realize again that only a country which one has both lived in and contemplated can assume in the mind that special sort of solidity which no amount of mere sight-seeing can give it. Really to possess the Valley I should need both the cowboy's doing and my own looking—which is something no one, perhaps, has yet achieved for that particular region.

I am not by any means sure that I should like to try. The fact that I never have stayed long in any part of the monument country may be the consequence of a certain defensive reaction. There is a kind of beauty —and it is presumably the kind prevailing throughout most of the universe—of which man gets thrilling glimpses but which is fundamentally alien to him. It is well for him to glance occasionally at the stars or to think for a moment about eternity. But it is not well to be too continuously aware of such things, and we must take refuge from them with the small and the familiar. I am not among those who are said to have already hopefully registered their names as prospective passengers on the first experimental rocket which our military authorities send to the moon because I very much doubt that I should like to stay even long enough to prepare for the return trip. And there is a certain suggestion of the lunar in the regions I have been contemplating.

According to the geologists, the sandstones which

compose them are quite young as rocks go—younger, for instance, than the uppermost layer of the Grand Canyon, below which the river has cut through successive strata to flow now over stone a billion years old. The limestone rim over which tourists peer was already formed while parts of Cathedral Valley were under water, and I myself have noticed, not far from it, a plain composed almost exclusively of shells which once belonged to quite up-to-date looking mussels. Yet for all that, the monuments look older than anything else on earth—partly perhaps because their age and the effects of it come within the scope of the human imagination, to which a thousand years are something conceivable while millions are not. It is certainly in part because they seem so old and so unchanging, so finished yet so nearly indestructible, that they are overwhelming and awesome.

Wherever the earth is clothed with vegetation not too sparse to modify its essential outlines, it makes man feel to some extent at home because things which, like him, change and grow and die have asserted their importance. But wherever, as in this region of wind-eroded stone, living things are no longer common enough or conspicuous enough to seem more than trivial accidents, he feels something like terror. Despite the stunted junipers and the harsh little shrubs upon which cattle can support themselves if they have space enough over which to wander, this is a country where the inanimate dominates and in which not only man but the very plants themselves seem intruders. We may look at it as we look at the moon, but we feel rejected. It is neither for us nor for our kind.

Here indeed is "beauty bare," and whoever has looked upon it may claim to have shared the experience which Miss Millay once attributed to Euclid alone. Certain cultures have, to be sure, tried to imitate it in their own creations. It is in the spirit of the pyramids, both Egyptian and Mayan. But they are a symptom of something deliberately destructive of that which those of us who are children of the Renaissance call "human," a symptom, that is to say, of a determination to live with and to be like something in which we really have no part.

As I climbed out of the vast emptiness up toward the heights where even snow and aspens seemed, by comparison, cozy and intimate, I tried to formulate in my own mind what it was that I had been most aware of as I stood in the shadow of one great block of sculptured stone to look across the clear air at another and another and another, towering in the distance. Perhaps what the landscape insisted upon was something which is only a little less obvious elsewhere. Perhaps it was only the platitude that man is small and that life is precarious.

But why should I say "only" a platitude? Art

knows no triumph greater than that which consists in making a platitude valid again. Why should it be assumed that nature herself can accomplish more? It was worth going to Cathedral Valley really to appreciate for an instant facts so often cited and so seldom realized. Perhaps it was also worth while to leave it soon. Such truths are among those which no one should either totally forget or be too constantly aware of.

# Chapter Sixteen

# Postscript

# Postscript

Despite my experience with nearly sixty of them, I have never yet learned how rapidly a year passes. "For a year" always sounds to me like "for keeps," and when I said "for a year and three months" that seemed very much like saying for "eternity—plus a little bit more." Now the year is gone and so too is a good part of the little bit more.

While the sun was crossing the sky three hundred and sixty-five times, the stars, hurrying just a little, crossed it three hundred and sixty-six. Though somehow I had never before thought of it just this way, this is of course what happens. Because the earth goes once all the way around the sun, it adds one additional apparent revolution of the starry sphere to the three hundred and sixty-five for which its rotation is responsible. Or, as perhaps those who figure such things out would prefer to say, it reduces by one the number of apparent voyages of the sun. In either event, a given constellation comes up nearly four minutes earlier (by sun or clock time) than it did the evening before and, frighteningly enough, four minutes a day adds up to twenty-four hours in a year.

Just as two clocks which do not keep the same time will nevertheless agree every so often when one has gained twelve hours over the other, so, once a year, sun time and star time are the same. A sun day is, alas, short enough, but a star day is shorter. Or would it, perhaps, be more cheerful to say that we get one more star day per year? That would at least constitute a reason which astronomers never give when defending their preference for siderial time.

One of the first things I noticed when I came here was Scorpio, which is, next to Orion, the most spectacular constellation in our sky though insufficiently appreciated in New England, where it lies too low and is usually cut off by hills even if the horizon is not obscured in a haze of city lights and dust. Scorpio disappeared from my ken about the same time that the earthly scorpions hid themselves for the winter, and it does resemble them a good deal more than most constellations resemble the figures for which they are named. Now I see it again as dusk falls, upright in the southeastern sky, its long tail ending in a bright, two-pointed sting and Antares gleaming an angry red in the middle of its thorax.

I am told that the Papago Indians, whose reservation occupies part of my home desert, call one of the constellations The Hand of God. I imagine that it must be Scorpio because the five stars which for us represent the head might well be taken as five fingers and the long narrow body as a wrist or arm. The Indians synchronize their agricultural cycle by the appearance of God's hand in the sky, and that is a very sensible procedure since it provides, gratis, a perpetual calendar almost perfectly accurate for human purposes.

In the end, to be sure, the custom might prove that ultraconservatism won't do even in such fundamental affairs, because the wobble of the earth's axis will affect even the behavior of Scorpio in the course of a few thousand years, and to assume then that its appearance meant just what it had once meant would prove disastrous. Fortunately, however, so far as this particular threat is concerned, even conservative Indians change more rapidly than the stars; long before Scorpio could prove misleading the Papago culture will have succumbed to forces pleasantly suggested in a current story about one individual long famous among the whites as a weather prophet. One day he startled some admirers by responding to the usual question about the prospects by a definitive "I don't know." Pressed for the reason behind this sudden collapse of his powers he replied briefly: "Radio broke."

One may, as I have done, throw away the calendar, let the clocks run down, and refuse to take in a newspaper. But as long as one looks at the sky, the passage of time will announce itself and the stars will remind one that it is later than we think. Resentfully I notice that as dusk falls Cygnus is again twinkling above the horizon and that the Great Bear is again over to the left of Polaris. Of all the many things one can do nothing about, there is none more ineluctable than this. When the birds return, or the shrubs and trees bloom again, there is some element of happy intention in those phenomena. "Here we are again," they say cheerfully. The stars say the same words, but in a different tone of voice. There is a hint of the implacable and the threatening: "Here *we* are *again*." And it is as though they meant to imply something more, something like "It makes no difference to us because we will be going 'round and 'round for a very long time still. It is only *your* revolutions, and *your* years that are numbered. Threescore and ten is not so many as to be difficult to count."

On the more trivial, more cheerful earth, the phenomena which I began to watch a little over a year ago are also beginning to repeat themselves and are now, for me, not novelties but expected things. When I heard this spring the first crowings of the white-winged dove I did not say this time, "What on earth is that" but only "Oh, so you are back at last." Before long now I shall probably, after some summer thunder shower, hear again out in the night-covered desert the odd bleatings of those spadefoot toads who startled me last summer and have, presumably, spent at least eight or nine months underground in some quiet quasi-hibernation. During the first year in any given place one is a visitor. As soon as things begin to come 'round again, one has begun to be a resident. And it was in order to become technically a resident that I settled here.

Also absent for the winter but back again now are the bats and the "bull-bats" who swoop in as night falls to catch invisible insects and to take water on the wing. The bats are of two sorts: one the California mastiff with, sometimes, a spread of twenty-one inches and therefore the largest of his kind in the United States; the other is the little Mexican free-tailed bat. Sometimes I benevolently turn on a floodlight to give them all an extra-good meal and to enable me at the same time to see that they are really taking something in the course of those apparently aimless swoops.

But the Mexican free-tailed bat serves also as a

kind of reproach. He reminds me of my most annoying piece of unfinished business—which will probably still be unfinished when I leave. It is the business, I mean, of his fellows at Carlsbad; why have they always, with one accord and ever since they first came under observation, spiralled out of their cave in a counterclockwise direction? In the beginning I assumed that it would only be a matter of asking the right person or, if I should be lucky enough to find that nobody knew, only a matter of making a few observations. Now I realize that though nobody seems to know the answer, parallel observations are not easy to make.

The problem, as readers may remember is this: Do all bats in the Northern Hemisphere go counterclockwise when they leave a cave with a vertical shaft and have to spiral to gain altitude? If so, is this because the earth spin gives them a slight impulse in this direction? I have talked to a good many people and written a good many letters addressed to bigger and bigger bigwigs because I hesitate to bother the biggest with questions which the less eminent could answer. Finally I got to Dr. Colin Campbell Sanborn of the Chicago Museum of Natural History, probably our greatest authority on bats in general. He not only answered me very courteously, but did a good deal more. He had the literature of the subject searched to find out if anything relevant had been recorded from America, Asia, or Africa. No one, he discovered, seems to 'have raised the question or noted even incidentally any telltale facts. "One finds the phrases 'dense masses,' 'long streams,' etc. but no mention of a spiral, clockwise or counterclockwise."

Turning in another direction I applied to Mr. Preston R. Bassett of the Sperry Gyroscope Company, who has been studying the general question of the effect of the rotation which, by the way, I learned is called the "Coriolis Effect." He has found, among other things, that it causes the western banks of streams flowing north-south to be higher and less shelving than the eastern ones. But of a possible effect on bats he had never heard. Mr. Edwin Way Teale gave me some good leads; the American Museum of Natural History expressed interest; the Park Department joined in; and Mr. William Schaldach, Jr., a young man who has been collecting the bats of this region for a museum, added one bit of information. He has noticed that when a bat has been shot it often falls in a clockwise spiral—which is presumably what should be expected if the Coriolis Effect really is being made manifest.

Despairing of being told, I made some efforts to get at least the beginning of an answer for myself and, among other things, followed a bad tip which took me on a trip of more than a hundred miles. But though there are lots of caves with bats and lots of mine shafts with vertical exits, the caves are not vertical and the vertical shafts don't seem to have bats. I am beginning to be a little discouraged about the whole business but I *still* think it is an interesting question.

I suppose I really hope the answer will be that, wherever the special conditions necessary prevail, Northern Hemisphere bats go counterclockwise and their southern relatives in the opposite direction. That would, at least, seem neat and definitive. On the other hand, since I am rather prone to hope that there is not a mechanical explanation for practically everything, it would also be gratifying to learn that there was positively nothing at all in my Coriolis Effect theory. One would then be left to wonder just how the Carlsbad community came to agree upon its traffic laws. Their convention is certainly a "socially useful one." Without it, a bat would find leaving the cave almost as dangerous as driving to work in a car.

Perhaps someday someone will turn a discarded wind tunnel on end and put a few hundred bats at the bottom of it. And if this sounds like an attempt to set up an apparatus for the solution of one of those "problems" of which I have spoken somewhat derisively, I can only say that, after all, one's own problems are always interesting. The bats have got into my belfry. And at least the unanswered question is an addition to the many other reasons why it might be nice to come back here again some day. I can already see my application to one of the foundations. Proposed Project: "A Study of the Coriolis Effect in Relation to Bat Flight."

"Come back here again someday." Such phrases have not occurred to me very often during the past year and the fact that this one falls naturally now means something. Hope is a cheerful thing but it also has sad implications.

Somewhere it has been said that no one ever thinks of the end of a holiday before it has begun. Conversely, when one does begin to think of "next time" one is nearing the end of the present. But at least I have accomplished what students of educational psychology call "the primary objective." I have stayed in a strange place long enough to observe the process by which the strange is transformed into the familiar. When I get back to what was once familiar it will seem strange in its turn.

Is that good or bad? Granted that what one wants is to be acutely aware both of the fact that one is living and of the facts of the world one lives in, should one scorn the easy stimulus of novelty? Should one therefore do absolutely all of 'one's traveling in Concord? I am familiar with Thoreau's answer to that question, as well as with his not absolutely consistent practice. Casting about for other testimony on the subject, preferably in a different context, I remember St. Augustine.

The author of *The City of God* took a very dim view of pilgrimages, even to holy places. In a sermon against the then current mania for just such jaunts—which were perhaps not always as serious in intention as they pretended to be—he wrote, in that rhetorical, epigrammatic fashion learned from his profane Roman predecessors: "*Noli longa itinera meditari; ubi credes, ubi venis; ad enim, qui ubiqui est, amando venitur, non navigando.*" His adjuration might be completely secularized and freely rendered somewhat as follows: "Do not plan long journeys because whatever you believe in you have already seen. When a thing is everywhere, then the way to find it is not to travel but to love." Certainly the essence of what I have been looking for is present in New England no less than in Arizona, and certainly only by loving can it be found in either place.

A considerably more recent and considerably less grave writer, Mr. E. V. Lucas, has something to say which might be interpreted as an argument on the same side. "Many of us," he says, "are so constituted that we never use our eyes until we are on foreign soil. It is as though a Cook's ticket performed an operation for cataract." But perhaps that is really on the opposite side of the argument, since a secular writer may accept human weakness as a premise more freely than a sacred one may.

Many of us are indeed "so constituted." Perhaps an ideal Thoreau would not have gone to Cape Cod or the Maine woods. Perhaps everything in the universe implies everything else, and I should know the desert by the swamp, the cactus by the skunk cabbage. But I don't, quite. My weakness is such that I have, to put it mildly, profited from living where nature manifests herself in ways that are striking because they are unfamiliar. The early Christian who pleaded his weakness to St. Augustine and protested that he believed more firmly in the Resurrection after he had seen the Holy Sepulcher would probably have got short shift. I imagine that the ghost of Thoreau is more indulgent.

Only yesterday I saw a road-runner crossing a patio to an artificial pool and I thought he was looking for a drink. But he had, as I presently learned, other plans. A huge red dragonfly zoomed over the water and, quick as a flash, the clumsy-looking bird leaped two feet into the air, seized the insect neatly in his bill, and stalked triumphantly away, presumably headed for a nest full of young under some creosote bush in the desert. Just because I had never seen that before, I saw it more completely than I shall

ever again see a robin extracting a worm from my
Connecticut lawn. If, in the end, it comes down to
much the same thing, why then it is only by observing much that one can realize how invariably that is
what it does do—come down to the same thing. Or
as a philosopher might put it, the human mind can
appreciate the One only by seeing it first as the Many.

Cervantes says something about the desirability of
considering things in the Dry as well as in the Wet.
Perhaps I have taken him a bit overliterally, but that
is exactly what I have been trying to do. And if I
have confirmed my conviction that, for me at least,
nature, wet or dry, furnishes the most cheerful as
well as the most intelligible context for thinking
and living and being, that is all I had hoped for.
Whether the gods approve the depth and not the
tumult of the soul, I am not prepared to decide, but
I am at least sure that I do. It is said that some ex-
cessively prudent people are forsaking cities entirely
in the hope of thus escaping the effects of atomic
explosions, but if I should ever follow their example
it would be rather because I wanted to preserve some
sanity of mind and spirit until the bomb fell.

To one kind of saint, all the visible manifestations
of nature, animate or inanimate, are included in that
world which is "too much with us." To me it seems,

on the contrary, that this particular world has become increasingly too little, not too much, "with us."
And to believe as I do, one does not need to believe
that nature embodies any ideal rightness. It is
equally true if one believes, instead, that she illustrates the fundamental contingencies of things-as-
they-are and that those who forget to observe her
are pretty sure to act with disastrous disregard of the
contingencies which she illustrates.

Since she is joyous, it is a great mistake to forget
how to share in her joy. Since she also accepts much
that is unacceptable to men who have pushed too
far in their efforts to imagine a universe they think
they would like better, it is also a great mistake to
forget completely how to reconcile ourselves, as she
does, to things unreconcilable with purely human
attitudes. In any man-made world one still meets
them pretty frequently, most frequently of all, perhaps, in the most crowded, most "civilized" communities. If the scheme of things is a "sorry scheme,"
man's attempts have not brought it very close to the
heart's desire.

What I learned from my desert year was, first and
most generally, to be "more sure of all I thought was
true." Specifically, I re-learned many platitudes, including some I have mentioned—such as, for instance, that courage is admirable even in a cactus;

that an abundance of some good things is perfectly compatible with a scarcity of others; that life is everywhere precarious, man everywhere small.

And of course I learned also one platitude more: Wherever one goes one has one's self for company.

Some other books published by Penguin
are described on the following pages.

*Gerald Durrell*

## FILLETS OF PLAICE

Gerald Durrell the humorist meets Gerald Durrell the naturalist in this sampler of escapades from his adventures.
Beginning with "The Birthday Party," Durrell takes us back
to the Corfu of *My Family and Other Animals*. From the
wildlife-collecting days of *A Zoo in My Luggage* comes a
slapstick episode to rival the wildest imaginings of Lewis
Carroll. And Durrell appears here under new guises too—as
a young man in love with a boisterous Miss Malaprop, and
in a hospital for a "rest cure" that nearly becomes a riot. "A
feast of laughter," said *Publishers Weekly*, "a delightful
and satisfying volume."

## CATCH ME A COLOBUS

*Catch Me a Colobus* catches Gerald Durrell in three of his
finest (and often funniest) roles—zoo keeper, ecologist, and
animal lover. Reaching new anecdotal heights, he writes
about escaped chimpanzees, a lioness in labor, and the
hazards of breeding rare creatures like the colobus monkey
and the teporingo. He also recounts his exciting expedi-
tions to Sierra Leone and Mexico in search of such en-
dangered species, which he hopes to perpetuate in his own
zoo. Like his other books, this one brings readers amazingly
close to the wildlife that is Durrell's major concern. Illus-
trated by Edward Mortelmans.

*Gerald Durrell*

## A ZOO IN MY LUGGAGE

This is a hilarious account of how Gerald Durrell founded his own private zoo. Durrell and his wife travel to the Cameroons and, helped by the renowned Fon of Bafut, manage to collect "plenty beef." Their difficulties begin when they find themselves back at home with Cholmondeley the chimpanzee, Bug-eye the bush-baby, and various other animals . . . and nowhere to put them.

## THE WHISPERING LAND

Durrell roams the Argentinian wilds in search of additions to his zoo. Besides meeting guanacos and rheas on the pampas, he encounters quantities of macaws, parrots (one of them with a treacherous flow of abuse), seriemas, and other birds, as well as mammals like a half-starved ocelot and a peccary with pneumonia.

## MENAGERIE MANOR

The riotous story of the growth of Durrell's zoo. With the help of his enduring wife, selfless staff, and reluctant banker, the zoo expands amid the capers of a tapir, the romance of a gorilla, the idiocy of a gray-winged trumpeter, and the antics of various orangutans, lions, bears, porcupines, and other creatures.

## THE CREATION

### Photographs by Ernst Haas

This beautiful book depicts the earth as it might have looked on the day of its creation. One of the world's great photographers, Ernst Haas believes that no medium today can interpret nature better than the camera. His point is proved by the magnificent color plates in *The Creation*: mysterious reflections of mother-of-pearl, eerie rock formations, foaming waters, spectral forests, flamingos in flight, elephants silhouetted against a setting sun, and many other scenes of strange, antediluvian beauty. An introduction and the opening passages of the Book of Genesis precede the photographs, which are followed by Haas's notes on where and how he took them. "[Haas] is a free spirit, untrammeled by tradition and theory, who has gone out and found beauty unparalleled in photography."—Edward Steichen.

## BUTTERFLY MAGIC

### Photographs by Kjell B. Sandved
### Text by Michael G. Emsley

The iridescent beauty of the butterfly has never been more colorfully captured than in this book of photographs by Kjell Sandved. Especially dramatic are Sandved's breathtaking enlargements of butterfly wings, which run across many of the pages like brilliant abstract paintings. Michael Emsley's text describes the life of the butterfly—how it communicates, how it finds its mate, how it escapes its enemies—and *Butterfly Magic* concludes with notes on the different characteristics of all the species photographed.